finding time

Breathing Space for Women Who Do Too Much

Paula Peisner Coxe

SOURCEBOOKS, INC.
NAPERVILLE, ILLINOIS

Published by Sourcebooks, Inc.
P.O. Box 4410, Naperville, Illinois 60567-4410
(630) 961-3900
FAX: (630) 961-2168
www.sourcebooks.com

Library of Congress Cataloging-in-Publication Data
Coxe, Paula Peisner
 Finding time : breathing space for women who do too much
/ by Paula Peisner Coxe.—3rd ed.
    p. cm.
 ISBN 1-4022-0250-4
1. Women—Time management—United States. I. Title.
HQ1221.C7555 2004
640'.43'082—dc22

                                    2004001367

        Printed and bound in the United States of America
           VP   10   9   8   7   6   5   4   3   2   1

It is not how much we do,
but how much love we put in the doing.
It is not how much we give,
but how much love we put in the giving.
Mother Teresa

Table of Contents

To many activities and
people and things.

Too many worthy
activities, valuable things
and interesting people.

For it is not the merely
trivial which clutter our lives,
but the important as well.

—Anne Morrow Lindbergh

Introduction

I recently read *Finding Time: Breathing Space for Women Who Do Too Much* again with the hope of updating its contents for this new, third edition. Just more than a decade has passed since this book was first published and I find that the time-saving tips and inspirational ideas still ring true today. While I have added several new chapters, the time-saving tips are intended to be timeless, though much has happened in the past decade. As you know all too well, the blistering pace of everyday life seems to speed up with every passing year. With advances in technology intending to make our days richer, easier and fuller—Blackberries, Palm Pilots, and instant messaging, to name a few, our senses are senselessly stimulated like never before. Sure, cell phones, voice mail, email, pagers, drive-thrus, same-day delivery, and ATMs help us find short-cuts, ways to shave a few minutes off our day. Yet, with this abundance of technology meant to make our lives more convenient, we are still stressed, taking some amount of pride in our "busyness" as we breathlessly rush about. Truly, no amount of new technology eases the burden of our busy days.

Why?

Being busy is the problem. Cherishing the moment is the solution.

To "be busy" has become synonymous with being productive, purposeful, and prolific. However, in reality, being busy is a symptom of something closer to home. Busyness is evidence of losing control of that which is important (meaning, purposeful) and placing unfulfilling importance on the unimportant (mindless, low value.) Being busy is reactive—responding to the demands, pressures, requests, and responsibilities of daily life. Think of it as a yo-yo or a ping pong ball, back and forth, pulled, prodded, and pushed. You as a yo-yo.

Oh, no!

By picking up this book, you are embarking on a path to take back your life, to spend your time and energy on what is important to you by controlling and conserving time, by working smart, not hard, by slowing down to cherish the moment. True, there are only so many hours in our pressure-packed days with much to accomplish. Let's take a moment to reflect on this pressure. Time pressure—it's the pinch to get everything off our list. The need to say "yes" to everyone who needs us. The desire to give of ourselves, often at our own expense. The urge to do as much as possible in the shortest time span to please others, to do what is right, to do what we are responsible for. Yet, when do we have the time to breathe—to relax, work out, read, or simply do nothing—we seldom seem to benefit from the fruits of our labor.

We, as women, shouldering the many responsibilities of home, family, friends, and work, always have something to do: children, house projects, the office, parents, volunteering, church or temple, and neighborhood activities. We spend much of our time caring for others and are happy to do so. Often, we go to bed breathless, feeling drained, dizzy, even overwhelmed. We don't even cherish our sleep, waking up tired and anxious, let alone appreciate that which we have accomplished during the day. The world can feel like a spinning top as we try to keep from falling.

If you're like me, you often wish you could scale back the noise, slow down the race, even step aside and become a spectator—if only for a moment. That wish sent me looking for time management books that might help me find more time. Back in 1992, I was disappointed. Most books were directed at understanding the psychology of time management or becoming highly efficient at the office. I wanted a book that was simple, easy to use, and had practical, timeless hints that would allow a woman like me to enrich her life by balancing its many aspects in a simple and real way.

Unable to find that treasure, I began collecting simple, common-sense tips from everyone I knew—my friends, family, and colleagues at the office. I also started identifying things that worked for me. Although I'm not an efficiency guru or academician, I have found ways to successfully manage my time and outside demands so I can enjoy my life more. The simple, practical tips you'll find in this book are intended to help you live your life to its fullest. Taken together, these tips form a wide menu of tools you can apply to your world. Be real with what makes you happy and with what you need to do to get there. Know your limits. Listen to your heart. Most of all, use the ideas and tips in this book to stimulate and inspire. Have fun with them. Try some, but let others go if they don't work for you. The worst thing you can do is stress about the "to-do" things in this book. Remember, keep it simple and real. This book is meant to help and heal, to reduce stress, not increase it.

Above all, I believe that time is both a precious and limited asset to be managed and controlled by each individual according to her purpose in life. Our lives are made up of many moments in time. Each of us has a purpose. Each of us has time to fulfill our purpose in life. In order to do so, time is not timeless and must be used wisely. Like money, time can be saved, invested, spent, made, multiplied, or wasted. How well you use your moments on this earth depends upon your perception of time's value. The habits you form and the commitment to be disciplined and mindful of the fleeting nature of this limited resource will make the difference. The easy-to-adopt habits that are presented in this book are designed to identify and eliminate the behaviors that rob us of these fleeting moments while replacing them with healthy habits to make the most of the time we are given on this earth.

I call the elements that rob you of time "time bandits." Time bandits are not only all around you, they are also within you. Saboteurs, they are the part of you that gets caught up in the moment and forgets to focus on the essential, that which is important. Time bandits are interruptions, other people's emergencies, needy acquaintances who focus on their needs, wants, and desires, not respecting the value of your own precious moments in time. The good news is that time bandits can be combatted with self-control. That's right: you're in charge. Others may impact your life or place demands on you, but it is up to you to take control, value your intuition, preserve your energy, set the right priorities, and use your God-given gifts wisely.

The secret to finding breathing space rests in developing habits that allow you to optimize the value of your personal life clock. That's what these tips do. Once you try them, you'll discover that twenty-four hours in a day is enough, that the time to do something is what's stretched, not you. You'll still spend time taking care of others and following through with your responsibilities, but you'll also have more time to take care of yourself. Yes, more time to take care of yourself. This deserves repeating.

A word of warning: this book is not about exploring theories of human behavior, why we need to please, be perfect, or any other type of psychobabble. This book is about consistently managing everyday demands that, if not controlled, rob you of precious hours. These healthy, life-affirming habits are not difficult to form, nor do they require abrupt changes in your life— unless you are a procrastinator. Some say real procrastinators have a deep-seated issue to deal with, such as fear of failure, fear of success, or a need to control. This may be true. However, it's not my goal to understand the procrastinator's motivation, nor the addictive, compulsive, perfectionist personality. Rather, this book is intended to help you differentiate between what you should do, what you want to do, and what you don't have to do. By keeping it simple and keeping it real, you can still get all you need done with breathing space to spare.

If you do have the time bandits under control, this book may help to fine-tune and affirm your already effective ways. Use the tips that fit your lifestyle and personal preferences and put aside the ones that don't fit comfortably with who you are.

In this updated version, I've added new tips and expanded the thirty-six tips from the second edition. I ask only one thing of you—please take time to read this book over a slow cup of coffee or tea, on a park bench, under the covers before bedtime, or any time when you're not rushed and can reflect on each idea, savor its significance to your life, and reaffirm how you can make it work for you. Mark the pages that resonate, the ideas that call to you. Go back to them over the course of a few days and make the connection, reflect on how you have adopted new and healthy habits to take back control of what is important and purposeful to you.

Finding time is about being good to yourself. Think of it as peace of mind—the ultimate gift you can give yourself. So take a deep breath and cherish this moment in time.

Best wishes and God's blessings to you,

Paula Coxe

San Clemente, California

How To Get The Most From This Book

- Do you feel like you spend your life running breathlessly from one crisis to another?
- Do you make yourself indispensable?
- Are you always available?
- Do you have a hard time saying "no"?
- Do you think you can do it better yourself?
- Do you clean before the cleaning person comes?
- Do you take on more than you can handle?

If you answered "yes" to one or more of these questions, give some thought to how you spend your time. What do your mornings, afternoons, evenings, and weekends look like? How does your overcrowded schedule make you feel? Try logging your time for a few days to see where it goes. Write down how you would like to feel and where you would like to be spending more of your time. Before you attempt any of the helpful hints that follow, take a few minutes to quietly reflect on where you are, where you want to be, and what you want to get out of this book.

Remind yourself of your goals as you read through these tips, and consider the value of each tip to your own particular blend of responsibilities. Adapt the ones you think will work for you in your particular situation, lifestyle, and with your unique personality, so they fit like a warm glove. Leave your guilt and worry at the door. Bring with you passion, faith, and desire. As you joyfully discover the beauty in slowing down, cherishing the moment, and conserving your energy for its best use, you will find that you will wind up doing what you love, loving what you do, and having time to enjoy it—all in the same twenty-four-hour day.

Manage Others' Expectations

Honesty is a selfish virtue.
Yes, I am honest enough.

—Gertrude Stein

Perception is reality.

Say it isn't so, but it is.

I believe this is one of the most important laws of human nature. It doesn't matter how perfectly or fully something was done. If it's not what someone expected, it might not satisfy.

The solution? Learn to manage others' expectations, their perceptions of how things should be, of how things will turn out. Integral to understanding someone else's perceptions is an ability to form similar standards and measures of outcome. For instance, understand what your boss means by saying something is good, complete, well done, or outstanding. Understand what your teacher wants in a report—the content, length, topics covered, and depth of analysis. Understand what is good, not good enough, and great. Your standards may not be the same as the recipient of your fine efforts and good intentions. That's OK. Just understand how she sees it.

Communication is the key to understanding. Ask questions. Make implicit assumptions explicit. Confirm and reconfirm. Here are some effective ways to manage expectations:

- Reconfirm objectives or deadlines. Ask, "What do you expect, specifically?" and, "When do you expect it done?" Have the other person verbalize her point of view or communicate in writing. Then state your understanding of the request so there is no misunderstanding.
- If you believe something is easy, why let on? Why not suggest that it's as hard as others might think? This buys you extra time since harder things usually take longer, and you may find you need the time to handle the unexpected bumps in the road that can accompany even the easiest task.
- Don't make promises until you thoroughly understand what you have to do, what impact the promise will have on your other commitments, and the importance of the promise to your own goals. Say "I'll get back to you" or "Let me think about it" before committing.
- If you're running late or think you could be late, call and let the other person

know. Nobody likes surprises of this kind. This way you are not breathlessly running into a meeting flustered and anxious. You have also demonstrated that you respect and are conscious of the time of others.

- In a situation with a deadline, remember Murphy's laws—"Everything takes longer than you think" and "If anything can go wrong, it will." Well, when things go wrong, disappointment follows. To avoid unnecessarily disappointing yourself and others, it's best to manage their expectations in advance. Overestimate the time the task will take and underestimate the results. When the final result is seen, they will be, at the very least pleased, and possibly ecstatic—but never disappointed. Resist the urge to say immediately, "No problem—I can handle it." You will quickly find yourself overcommitted and short on time.

- Feel comfortable saying "I'm sorry." More often than not, you mess up through no fault of your own—these things happen. Think of the words "I'm sorry" as relationship insurance—they diffuse emotionally charged situations and build bridges. Come to terms with the possibility that you may not be able to meet a person's expectations, and realize that, in most cases, a simple, heartfelt apology will smooth any ruffled feathers.

Most people want to make others happy so that people will think well of them. Remember that it's not the promise that creates lasting satisfaction, *it's the meeting of expectations that does*. Make the words "Let me understand what you want, specifically" second nature when you take on new responsibilities.

In the final analysis, your ability to make time for yourself is a function of managing others' expectations. When you manage and meet—or exceed—them, you've gained both an ally and some time in the process.

Habit-Forming Tip:

Ask yourself these questions:
- "Why do I want to do this?"
- "What do I want out of this situation?"
- "What do the other people involved want or expect?"–Keep your answers focused on results.
- "How can I meet their expectations and keep my sanity?"
- "Can I realistically promise to meet their expectations and get what I want out of the situation?"

A Little Padding
Never Hurt

Let us not go over
the old ground,
let us rather prepare
for what is to come.

—Marcus Tullius Cicero

Padding isn't always on your shoulders or chest. Time padding is how you give yourself an extra cushion of comfort to get something done and feel good about it. Padding can be quite easy. It's all about stretching, extending the time it takes to accomplish a task, drive a certain distance, or get things done.

After all, why rush? Rushing causes stress and decreased productivity, not to mention frayed nerves. Pad all your time estimates and you'll avoid being late, rushing unnecessarily, and disappointing someone. It's a great technique that works with family life as well as business and community activities.

The motto I live by is "Expect the unexpected." Stuff happens. No matter how well-intentioned you are and how great your plans, unanticipated detours dot your path in all you do. The only person you can control is yourself, not others. And you must rely upon others to get things done. So, expect that stuff will happen at the start and pad, pad, pad.

I've made it a habit to pad my time estimates. My consulting work involves teams. On one cost-reduction project, a team member owed me her section of the report. The report was due on the 21. Because she is notoriously late, I told her that the deadline for her submission was the 14—one week earlier. The early deadline meant she did not delay timely completion of the project, and I had time to prepare an excellent report with time to spare to get ready for the client presentation.

The trick, though, was telling her two weeks before her piece was due so she had the time to do it. First I had to anticipate how much time she needed to get her work done. Then I had to give her a completion date that, even with her habitual tardiness, would not delay or cause me to rush or work late to meet my commitments.

Building in time is even more important when several other people are involved. To set dates like this, you need to project the number of links in the chain required to complete an act. If three people are required to get something done, anticipate the time it will take each to complete her part and get it to you. Then you can pad the time by anticipating the additional delays caused by coordinating these activities.

Tracy, a thirty-something mother of two, pads her children's time. Fifteen minutes before the carpool arrives, she tells six-year-old Sara and seven-year-old Joshua that they have to put away their toys and be ready for gymnastics in five minutes. She knows that both children will take the full five minutes to get started. Then Sara and Joshua will ever so slowly put each toy away. It will take them another five to ten minutes just to do that. By allotting fifteen minutes for her children to get ready, Tracy doesn't have to hold up the carpool.

Another tip she uses helps when the children are absorbed in watching television or playing a competitive game. Instead of insisting that they stop immediately, Tracy gives them ten minutes to finish up and come to dinner. They usually comply promptly.

Here are some padding techniques:

- Brownie Baking—Add up the hours it would take to do a project under perfect conditions. Then estimate how long it will take if you are interrupted or swayed off course. Use the higher estimate and add in a fudge factor before you commit to a deadline.

- The Fix-It—Figure out how many people are involved in getting the project done. Assuming their work will be late or incomplete, estimate the time required to fix it, and, working backwards from the project deadline, determine the individual deadlines.
- Complicate—Think about how you would get something done in its most complex, detailed version. Allow the amount of time it would take to complete the task in this way, but let it be done in its most simplified way.
- Expect the unexpected—at all times!

One final note: Padding is intended for situations you can control. Use it where it makes sense. If there is no room in your schedule for slack, you can throw padding out the door. In other words, pad when it fits.

Habit-Forming Tip:

A cushion of comfort pads you in the right place. Always extend your estimate of the time that's required to accomplish your goal. Do this for yourself as your own internal yardstick, and estimate time requirements for all the links in the chain.

Learn to Say No to Others and Yes to Yourself

I must govern the clock,
not be governed by it.

—Golda Meir

You have legitimate rights, needs, desires, and dreams. And, ultimately, you want to feel satisfied and bring satisfaction to others by completing what you have agreed to do and by doing what you want to do. Be good to yourself. Learn how to break the mental pattern of believing "They need me" and "I can't say no." *Only when you accept the right to set boundaries can you live your life on your own terms.* More importantly, you will gain peace of mind and a sense of security in knowing that you are not overcommitted, overburdened, and overwhelmed—that busy is not better. Often we equate rejection with being told "no." Rejection is uncomfortable. A friend of mine recently shared some valuable advice. He said that before you say or do something that makes you feel unsure or uncomfortable, ask yourself three questions:

Is it kind?

Is it necessary?

Is it true?

This puts saying "no" into perspective.

Recognizing the possibilities of "no" is the first step. The consequences of agreeing to something that is impossible or impractical are significant. I'm sure you've been through this scenario: You agree to do something that a little voice inside you says you shouldn't. Maybe you can't do it comfortably, completely, or on time. Maybe you are so overcommitted that the new thing you agree to take on won't even be enjoyable, although it could be. In the end, your gut feeling was right, and you wind up with a disappointed husband, child, friend, family member, neighbor, or business associate. You are then cast in the role of being inconsiderate, making someone wait, dropping the ball, doing it halfway, or not caring enough.

Sometimes it's better to say "no." That's right, don't do it. By learning to say "no" without justifying yourself to a spouse or feeling guilty to a child, you reclaim your life, your peace of mind, and, most importantly, your sanity. That said, keep in mind that "no" can be communicated in many ways, and some ways are much less harsh and alienating than others. Here are some examples of how to sugarcoat a "no":

- I can do it another time: "I would love to do this for you, Bill, but I've got two other commitments for Wednesday and Thursday. If you need it done, I can do it by next Tuesday. I can't do it tomorrow."
- If only I had known in advance: "I'd like to help you out, but I've got myself involved in this family dinner and I just can't do it this time. If I had known about this a couple weeks earlier, I could have planned around it. I'm sorry."
- I'll arrange for someone else: "I won't be able to make it that day. Why don't I call Carol and Bonnie to see if they can go?"
- I'll get back to you: "Let me check my calendar. I'll get back to you."
- I'm busy that day: "I think I'm already committed, but I'll let you know."
- I can do some of it: "If we have to meet Wednesday's deadline, I can do the methods and procedures, but the policy write-up will have to wait until the next

report. We can't have it all complete by Wednesday. Do I have the priorities right or should we switch them around? Now, I'm assuming the Wednesday deadline is an inflexible date."

In some of these examples, you can see that I'm not really saying "no." I'm saying I can't meet an impossible deadline. Or, I can meet the deadline with two out of three things you want. Or, I could have done it if I'd had more notice. Or, I can't do it, but I can help find someone who will. It's still "no," but because it's sugarcoated, it's easier to swallow. And you still get to set the boundaries that bring you peace of mind.

I haven't mentioned one important thing. Many times, you can't say "no" because of your need to be in control. You see, if you wind up doing everything, you satisfy your need to be in charge, not depend on anyone else, and be in a position of knowing that it is done right. A soulful introspection will uncover why you have a hard time saying "no." If it's based on the need to be in control, recognize that learning to surrender, trust, and depend on others brings its own rewards. Suffice it to say that it's a good idea to assess the motives behind the pleaseaholic personality and understand if it applies to you.

The basic principle here is acknowledging and accepting that it's OK to say "no." You have that choice. If you recognize how much room you have to maneuver, you can make time. Say "no" to others and "yes" to yourself. By setting boundaries with dignity, you shed the need to please in favor of pursuing priorities that bring pleasure and satisfaction. Most importantly, you recognize the power of words to create or to destroy. By choosing your words wisely, saying "no" when "no" is necessary is OK.

Habit-Forming Tip:

When somebody asks you to do something, pause before answering. Don't rush to comply. If you have to say "no," do it effectively and sugarcoat it. Make your pause instinctive. Give yourself time to think. If the situation is too emotionally charged for a face-to-face response, use voice mail or email to say "no." It may seem like a cowardly way out, but it gets the point across and doesn't leave anyone hanging in the balance. Listen to your instincts and understand your true motives. If "no" is the right answer, say so.

Sometimes it's best to let go when you know you can't make it. To continue on would be fruitless and to stop would be like giving up. So, why not punt? Let go of the ball and let someone else have a turn at it. Maybe you didn't have enough time to complete what you set out to do, or maybe there were more obstacles than you had anticipated. Whatever the reason, know that it's OK to let go.

One way to punt is to say, "I can't do this," and ask for help. It's not a sign of weakness. Offer alternatives like:

> I'm sorry, Susan. I won't be able to pick up Gia next Tuesday. My mother-in-law is coming into town. I think Risa could pick up Gia because her daughter has a dance lesson nearby. Can I call her for you?

Here are some hints on effective punting:
- Give yourself and others enough time to punt. Don't wait until the eleventh hour.
- Know what you are up against so you can determine whether you

should punt or if you can really get it
done.

- Figure out alternatives on how, who,
  where, and when it can be done by
  someone else.
- Examine alternatives before offering
  them. Will they really work?
- Anticipate surprises and recognize
  when they're brewing.
- Recognize that it is a sign of strength,
  not weakness, to know what you
  don't know and understand what you
  can and can't do.
- Focus on results when you punt so
  the other person knows you are
  working toward a solution for them
  and not ducking your responsibilities.

You can only punt when your eyes are on
the ball. Be honest with yourself when you
may not be able to keep all your commit-

ments. Look a week or two ahead to see what is coming up. When you're sure conflicts will arise, contact the people involved and give them constructive alternatives. It's best to let someone down with enough advance notice so they can do something about it.

〜 Tip 4 〜

Build Solid Time Blocks—Limit Interruptions

A distraction is to avoid the consciousness of passage of time.

—Gertrude Stein

World-class athletes in action exhibit an uncanny ability to focus. They have the gift of "keeping their eyes on the ball." Champions do this by blocking out any distraction that will interrupt their concentration.

Unlike a game, life is not played in a controlled environment: the baby screams, the telephone rings, a friend pops in, a crisis erupts. However, you can control your environment by limiting interruptions during periods when you have your mind set on getting something done. Interruptions steal your time without remorse. It is perfectly legitimate to treat interruptions as rude time bandits. You can let people know that they are taking up your time in an assertive, yet polite, way.

The top three interruptions are: 1) yourself, 2) the phone, and 3) other people. Many interruptions are self-inflicted, such as daydreaming, snacking, nodding off, abandoning an important item to pursue a trivial one, or doing something fun like exercising or taking a bath when these activities should really be the reward after you've accomplished your goal. Surfing the Net is the reward after you have completed your project on the computer. You can minimize this by admitting you do it and saying, "It's OK, I'm human and I make mistakes. But I'm sick of this. I'll postpone the interruption because I'm in control here." By taking responsibility and focusing on tasks at hand, you enrich your life and add hours to your days.

The second main interruption you encounter on a daily basis is the telephone. You can control incoming calls by using an answering machine to screen them or having someone take messages. You can also learn key techniques to shorten an incoming call, which will be discussed in more detail in Tip 5. Outgoing calls are easier to manage because you make the call, you start the conversation, and you can limit its length and content.

The third top interruption is other people: the relative who drops by, the coworker who stops in to chat, the child who demands your attention, the client who needs your help all the time, and the friend with no impulse control who has to talk to you whenever the mood strikes. To limit these interruptions, let them know you would like to deal with what they want, that it's important to you, and that you'll specifically make time for it, but not now—unless you can handle the request on the spot.

There is nothing wrong with establishing a closed-door policy for a given amount of time to help get things done without interruption. The main point here is to limit interruptions by first recognizing them as interruptions, then taking control of the situation so you can continue to focus on the task at hand. Handle and end the interruption. Assess whether what the person wants can be handled quickly. If so, do it.

Here are a few ways to handle interruptions:

- Set a time limit: "Jim, that sounds good, but I've got to leave in a couple of minutes. Can you tell me about it briefly?"
- Set an appointment that you can control: "Sally, it's so good to see you. I

do want to talk about that snag in registration with you. I'm in the middle of something I have to get out within the hour. Are you free at 2:30 P.M. today? I'll come by your place." Or, "Jessica, Mommy is busy now. Go finish watching the video and I'll come to your room at four o'clock so we can fix the dollhouse."

• Close the door: "Sorry, John, I can't talk with you now. I'm holed up trying to finish this report. I'll call you tomorrow."

Beware of regular distractions that can interrupt, such as a loud TV, a churning washing machine, a dishwasher, or a barking dog. Noise can disrupt your concentration. By treating it as an interruption, you limit its ability to rob you of your time and mental energy. For, as we all know, there is only so much time and energy to go around.

Marion, a mother of five, values the uninterrupted time she finds after nine o'clock at night. She pays bills, does the wash, and makes lists. To her, "ten minutes in the evening is worth twenty-five minutes in the morning." Like Marion, if you take advantage of the uninterrupted time in your life and, if possible, create more, you will add unimaginable hours to your days.

Habit-Forming Tip:

Recognize that when an interruption occurs, it steals your time without asking. Be kind to yourself, the person on the phone, or other intruders, but be firm and stick to your schedule. When you are your own worst enemy and find ways to put off doing something, just do the worst first and then go on to more fun things.

The Phone—Your Friend and Foe

...Sat in front of the telephone, staring at it, waiting for it to come to life, hoping, beseeching, lifting it from time to time to make sure it was not out of order.

—Edna O'Brien

It seems to have a life of its own. It can bring you cheer, sadness, joy, or frustration. It demands your attention even though it's an inanimate object. Its seductive powers rob you of precious moments—unless you learn to manage it.

Phones are everywhere. The ever-present cell phone has become an appendage to most, a necessity to some, and an unknown to few. There are restaurants that ban cell phones because of the noise pollution and invasion to others' sense of space and privacy. The surest way to keep unwanted interruptions at bay is to not carry your cell phone, or at least turn it off.

Here are some specific hints on ways to make the phone your friend without having to abandon it all together:

- Leave your answering machine on to screen calls or have someone screen them for you—an assistant at work, a family member at home.
- Have your assistant at work say, "She's not available right now," not, "Would you like me to interrupt?" You can still

be responsive without being available at all times.

- Schedule outgoing calls for one part of the day, and make them all at once.
- Call before lunch or late in the day. People prefer short conversations at that time.
- Call the other party back so you're in control—don't let messages pile up.
- When you call someone back at a time on which you have both agreed—say between 3 P.M. and 4 P.M.—don't allow yourself to be put on hold unless it's more important for you to talk and you know the person is on the other line.
- Determine how long you want a call to last, and time it with a stopwatch.
- Leave detailed messages for others and ask them to leave detailed messages for you so you will both be prepared when you talk.
- Develop conversation closers, such as: "What can I do for you?" "You must be busy, so I'll let you go," "Is there anything

else we need to go over?" "I'm sorry for sounding so hurried, but I'm working against the clock," "Before we hang up..." or "I've got someone in my office."

- Turn on the answering machine a few minutes before leaving the home or office to be able to depart on time.
- Use a car phone to make drive time productive.
- Use fax or email to save time on the phone.
- Meet by phone whenever you can to save drive time for meetings that don't need to be face-to-face.
- Do other things while you are on hold—be productive.
- Consider taking advantage of convenient features such as automatic redial, speaker phones, speed dialing, call waiting, call forwarding, and conference calling.
- If you don't have time to chat, call someone when you know they aren't there and leave a message.

It's easy to lose track of time on the phone. Be aware of the time you're spending on the call and take pride in quality, not quantity.

The phone does not have to be a time bandit if you learn effective ways to control conversations. In fact, the phone can be one of your best time savers when you use it wisely. You can get many things done by phoning instead of driving to a store or waiting in traffic. My cousin uses the phone for everything:

I do a lot by phone whenever possible. I use my credit card to order flowers, balloons, tickets, or other special gifts. I try to use the stores that keep my credit card on file. I have a list of phone numbers for all those stores by the type of merchandise that I regularly buy from them. This list is my one-stop shopping.

Habit-Forming Tip:

- Your answering machine can screen calls to save time.
- Increase the productivity of each minute by multi-processing—doing more than one thing while you're on the phone.
- Be aware of the time spent on each call.
- Set aside time to make outgoing calls. By initiating the call, you will be better prepared and can control its pace and content.
- Use effective conversation closers.

∽ Tip 6 ∾

Be Reachable

Without discipline,
there's no life at all.

—Katharine Hepburn

"She's in a meeting."

"She just stepped out."

"She's off for the rest of the day."

How many times have you wanted to reach someone you know is on this planet, but is nowhere to be found? There's really no excuse for being out of touch. Cell phones, pagers, email, and answering machines make us reachable. In fact, new technology makes it pretty tough to hide.

Why is being reachable important? It saves time and avoids the buildups and complications of loose ends, unanswered questions, and confused people left to their own devices. Staying in touch simplifies.

Every now and then, it is necessary to go undercover—you must leave the answering machine on, turn the cell phone off, and focus on the tasks at hand without interruptions. Yet, being responsive is important. Strive to return emails and calls the same day. Doing so lets callers know they are important enough to be responded to in a timely and considerate manner.

Everyone wants to feel important. When you're out of touch, people think they don't matter to you, that they can wait. Being too busy says, however unintentionally, "You're not important to me." It's hard to believe that someone is too busy to get back to a friend, colleague, or relative the same day. Even if you don't have an answer for them, you can acknowledge receiving the call.

Here are a few hints on how to keep in touch and be reachable:

- Use a cell phone.
- Call everyone back the same day they called you.
- Give your travel itinerary to people who depend on you at home and at work.
- Respond in an email instead of a phone call.
- Use a pager.
- Leave detailed messages on how, when, and where you can be reached for a callback. Leave all your phone numbers: home, cell, office.

- Regularly check email messages at
  scheduled times of the day.

By being considerate and responsive, you gain the freedom to be where you want to be rather than where you have to be. Whether you're on the golf course, shopping at a mall, or in your home, be accessible. *Access is comforting*. Things get done that way.

Habit-Forming Tips:

- Make it a habit to check your messages and get back to people immediately—even if you don't have an answer. People will feel important because you took the time to be so responsive.
- Be reachable whenever possible—it's easier to handle things as soon as they happen.

Help Your Family
Help Themselves

Learn to get in touch
with silence within yourself
and know that everything
in this life has a purpose.
There are no mistakes, no
coincidences. All events are
blessings given to us
to learn from.

—Elisabeth Kubler-Ross

While we all want to feel needed, there comes a time when you have to stop doing things for others at the expense of yourself and let others learn to care for themselves. This doesn't mean that you are abdicating your role as caretaker. It means you are giving your family a great gift—the ability to be responsible and self-reliant.

Think about it. In your house alone, you are probably responsible for doing, arranging for, or coordinating more than thirty activities:

- baby-sitting
- bathing children
- buying clothes for kids and spouse
- buying presents and cards for birthdays and holidays
- caring for your aging parents
- cleaning rooms
- cleaning up after pets
- cooking
- disciplining
- dishwashing
- driving kids to school
- dusting

- feeding family
- feeding pets
- gardening
- going to the dry cleaners
- grocery shopping
- helping the kids with schoolwork
- keeping medical and financial records
- keeping tabs on items running low
- laundry
- maintenance of appliances and household items
- managing finances
- organizing parties and family events
- paying bills
- picking up after the family
- planning menus
- organizing children's play
- ordering catalog items
- mopping floors
- cleaning windows
- sorting and opening mail
- taking pets to the vet
- vacuuming

- volunteering at kids' school
- washing cars
- watering plants

Reading this list has probably left you breathless and possibly even speechless. Here are some ways to breathe easier and help your family to help themselves:

- Designate a spot where each family member can place dirty laundry. Have them put their own clothing in the hamper.
- Store individual-sized snack foods where kids can get them so you don't always have to prepare snacks from scratch.
- Trade off cooking nights with your husband and older children.
- Keep a chalkboard or hanging pad of paper in a regular place for everyone to write down items that are running low, that they need to buy, or that need to be fixed. Check the list before you run errands or go grocery shopping.

- Have a weekly or monthly calendar set up in clear view (perhaps by the refrigerator) where each family member can look to see what chore he or she has to do—set the table, empty trash, wash dishes, do laundry. Divide tasks fairly, allowing each member to do what he or she prefers, when possible.
- Store kitchen items in a designated place so time is not wasted searching for misplaced items.
- Show your family members how to use the microwave.
- Invest in a large freezer to store prepared foods for your family.
- Set aside time for a group meeting with family members to discuss how to solve common problems.
- Make a regular time each week to compare calendars with your spouse and kids and coordinate activities.
- Do things less frequently—instead of washing the bed sheets every week, try

every other week; instead of going grocery shopping every three or four days, go once a week and buy enough to last seven days.

- Let go of the need to do things perfectly—let family members do their best, even though it may not be done the way you would do it.

Allowing your family to take care of themselves gives you time to take care of yourself—to simply relax, read a book, do nothing, or get something done for yourself. Don't feel guilty about this. After all, if you don't take care of yourself, who else will?

Habit-Forming Tip:

Develop ways for family members to contribute to household chores, such as cooking, cleaning, grocery shopping, doing laundry, and running errands, knowing all the while that things don't have to get done exactly the way you would do them.

Brushing Your Teeth Isn't Fun, It's Necessary

Growth is the only
evidence of life.

—John Henry, Cardinal Newman

I never really look forward to brushing my teeth. But, because it's a habit, I just do it and don't think twice.

Well, the secret to creating more breathing space and time to enjoy life is to plan your time as regularly as you brush your teeth. By making it a habit to inventory your responsibilities and commitments, you'll get more done—in less time than ever.

Start by setting aside time every evening to list the things you need to do the following day. (If you're a morning person, you can set your goals at the start of each day.) Reflect on how you might best approach the tasks you've listed. The next morning, check your to-do list first thing and consult it regularly throughout the day to keep yourself on track. Each time you finish an item, give yourself a little pat on the back.

At the end of the day, congratulate yourself for the work you've done. You'll be pleasantly surprised at how much you've accomplished! Add items you didn't complete to the next day's list, but take a minute to think about why you didn't get around to them.

Like brushing your teeth, the process of planning, checking, and reviewing your obligations should take no more than a few minutes out of your day. Here's how to make it a habit.

First, get together an organizing system that works for you. Maybe it's a simple pad of paper or a Palm Pilot. Whatever you choose, create a format for your to-do lists. To start your first list, put down everything you can think of that needs to be done—impending birthdays, business projects, personal phone calls, letters, whatever. Don't worry if you don't get everything. Just add items as you remember them throughout the day.

Now, assign each a priority and get started! Cross off items as you complete them, and add the ones you haven't completed to tomorrow's list. Give yourself a moment of reward for getting things done. There's always another day to do the rest!

You should eliminate those tasks or activities that never seem to get done. They obviously aren't that important. I bet you'll be surprised at the progress you'll make. Chances are, few tasks will be on your list more than two or three days.

You may want to use the "self-co-optation" technique described by Tom Peters (*In Search of Excellence, Thriving on Chaos*) in which you arrange meetings with yourself, setting aside the time as though it were an appointment in your daily schedule. You can meet with yourself at the breakfast table, on the bus, or even in the bathtub. It's your time.

Don't forget to put leisure activities on your list, too. After all, you deserve rewards for your accomplishments. Save your daily to-do lists for a while, review them later on, and you'll be amazed at how much you've accomplished—and how much time you have to spare.

Habit-Forming Tips:

Do a to-do list daily. Don't write a new list every day, just update the previous one. Prioritize the list. Combine some tasks; eliminate others. Be sure to include your leisure activities as time for you. Continue the process to look at your progress. And reward yourself for all you do! Don't forget to be good to yourself on those days when you're on overload. Hide the list until tomorrow—it will still be there waiting for you.

First Things First: It's a Matter of Priorities

**Do every act of your life
as if it were your last.**

—Marcus Aurelius

Do you ever wonder how a juggler does it? With several balls in the air, how does she keep the momentum and even add balls along the way? Well, her first priority is the first ball that touches her hand. She catches it and throws it up at the exact angle and height that enables it to fall in her hand at precisely the right moment. If she started looking at all the balls, she would lose focus, and the chain would be broken.

The same rule applies to your life. You have to decide what is most important, what comes next, and what can wait. Your sense of priority is based upon your perception of the consequences of your action or inaction. A number of questions can help you decide when an activity needs to take place, what is required, and what outcome is expected.

Ask yourself:

"Who will be disappointed?"

"Will we lose a deal?"

... and the Million-Dollar Question:

"What is the worst thing that can happen if I don't do this?"

Be honest with yourself, and determine your priorities based upon your answers. Give yourself a break. If it's not so important, don't do it. Eliminate things whenever possible. And remember that being perfect and doing too much when it really isn't necessary don't make for a happier you. It's far better to do less and enjoy the journey!

It takes mental discipline to set priorities. Often, you have to rethink your assumptions. It's not enough to simply ask the Million-Dollar Question. Use some form of the ABC priority system to rank activities in order of importance. The ABC priority system compartmentalizes activities into three areas: A–extremely important, B–important, and C–not important. A typical day might look like this:

A–Extremely Important
    Take daughter to doctor
    Complete tax forms for accountant
        meeting tomorrow
B–Important
    Clean house for guests tonight

Go grocery shopping
C–Not Important
    Buy birthday gift for Gail
    Go to post office
    Take car in for servicing

This method can be adapted in many ways to best suit your needs. For example, my friend Risa uses the ABC priority system, but puts a gold border around those things that produce money and a red border around other activities. The idea is to use the approach in a way that works for you.

Doing the most important things first allows you to plan your personal time. First, determine if something can be delegated. If it can't, then prioritize it. Establishing priorities takes into account deadlines, ease of completion, urgency, and others' expectations. In the final analysis, whether something is worth doing at all depends on the answer to the Million-Dollar Question: What is the worst thing that will happen if I don't do this?

In answering this question, honestly assess if the consequences are real or imagined. Often, we create the drama with performance expectations that are too high. As we all know in our hearts, we are harder on ourselves than anyone else could ever be.

When all else fails, remind yourself of the German proverb: One who begins too much accomplishes little.

Habit-Forming Tip:

Always ask yourself these five questions:
- Am I doing the most important things first?
- How urgent is this task?
- How can I get somebody else to do the task for me?
- What's the worst thing that can happen if I don't do this?
- Is the worst thing that can happen a real expectation or a drama of my own creation?

≈ **Tip 10** ≈

Schedule
Personal Time

It is good to have an end
to journey towards; but
it is the journey that
matters in the end.

—Ursula K. Le Guin

It's not enough to just fit fun in. Fun should be a priority, and it should be scheduled. At the end of your day, it's the time shared with those you care about that leaves an imprint on your heart. Fun is about creating memories—when moments stand still in time, when you wish it could last forever, when you laugh 'til your cheeks hurt, when you do things without purpose—just for the fun of it. It's about laughter, discovery, and just being together.

As Ben Franklin said, "Time is the stuff of which life is made." Your life is comprised of diverse interests: family, friends, work, spirituality, religion, culture, and physical and intellectual pursuits. You constantly juggle and try to balance these interests. It's up to you to find the balance in it all—the enjoyment of the process, of how you get to where you are going, is what creates a sense of wonder, excitement, joy, and satisfaction.

Although scheduling enjoyment sounds contradictory, that's exactly what you must do to really make time for it. Ask yourself this—when was the last time you took a long vacation, a really long one? Not just a three-day weekend or a short getaway combined with a business trip. I mean a *real* vacation where you have so much time that you are beginning to wonder what to do, where you have time enough to unwind, relax, and then get a little bored. In Europe, these vacations of four to six weeks are commonplace. In the U.S., you have to improvise. Maybe it's taking all three weeks in one long vacation and not splitting it up. Maybe it's scheduling little to do in a two-week vacation so you aren't running from museum to museum. Maybe it's going to a family spot where you can spend fun time with your children and build the best sandcastles ever imagined.

To make enjoyment a priority, figure out what fun means to you. Short of going on a long vacation, there are many things you can do in your everyday life that are fun and enjoyable and allow you to relax, recharge, laugh, and forget your worries. It may be playing tennis, shopping, reading a good book in the backyard, gardening, or painting. Think of the top three or four things that, if you had time, you'd love to do, but have put off for one reason or another. Now take the ones that are realistic, that you could do now if you had the time, and schedule them in your calendar this month. Yes, block out the time and make an appointment with yourself for fun.

Dorothy, a stockbroker, mother, and wife, puts it this way: "Pick something you like to do and that you feel deprived of if you don't do. Make an appointment with yourself to do it. It becomes an emotional commitment." Alan and Cathy, a married couple with two children, have a date night once a week. On Wednesdays, they go out and spend a quiet evening together, maybe dinner, movies, or simply a stroll. It's a rejuvenating time for them and they look forward to it every week.

How about setting aside one afternoon on the weekend to visit friends and maybe catch a movie? Block off the time and make it a priority. All work and no play makes for a boring, unhappy person. We all know at least one of these—breathless, no smile, harried, skirting by as she hurries to her next appointment. Without private time and a change of scenery, you lose perspective, your nerves fray, and you create drama where little may exist.

Know that you are worth it and that you must have private time to maintain your spirit and high energy. Make fun time spent with the ones you love precious to you. After all, this is what makes life worth living—the lives you touch—and the only way to touch is by spending time together, without agenda or occasion, without rushing. These are the kind of times that create memories and leave lasting impressions.

Other times, simply spending time alone is fun. Make a date with yourself. It's rejuvenating to be able to think uninterrupted, to dream wide awake, and to be pampered for all your hard work. Whatever form fun takes—be it a walk in the park, a facial or massage, a swim in the ocean—know it is essential to have some time alone to create a healthy and balanced you.

Of course, some limits do need to be set. Allowing yourself too much leisure time may result in wasting time, which will only create more stress. Carefully plan and schedule your personal time so that it is relaxing, fulfilling, and emotionally productive. In other words, sitting around procrastinating and worrying about all the things you have to do is not leisure time—that's wasting time. Make sure you take your time off when you will not be distracted by thoughts of what you "should" be doing. Accomplish your goals, then plan to reward yourself.

Don't make the mistake of so many who don't know how to have fun. Those who feel they are defined by their work can't relate to people and have a hard time being alone and hearing the beat of their own heart. Solitude and quiet offer opportunities for reflection and rejuvenation. Everybody deserves rest. Life demands of you that you do your work, and you need to demand of yourself that you make time to enjoy the fruits of your labor.

Here are a few ways to strengthen your spirit in your personal time:

- Go for a long, quiet walk
- Take a relaxing bubble bath with candlelight

- Read an inspirational book
- Make time to pray and talk to God
- Take a vacation
- Exercise
- Take a class in something you've always wanted to learn
- Pamper yourself with a facial, massage, or makeover
- Take yourself to dinner and a movie
- Buy yourself some new clothes or jewelry

Off-hours are precious. Make time for yourself and those you love so that you focus on the journey, not the end. How blessed are those who look back on a life well-lived and say, "It's been a great ride!"

Habit-Forming Tips:

- Get accustomed to scheduling all of your time.
- Give your own personal enjoyment a high priority. Plan ahead and schedule it.

Elephants Remember, People Don't

The brain is as strong
as its weakest think.

—Eleanor Doan

How often do you hear, "Let me check my calendar?" I bet the person who says that is in control of her life and knows her commitments before she makes another. She doesn't rely on memory. She writes down her commitments, plans, and priorities. So should you.

It's said that Sigmund Freud did not know his own phone number, because he felt that if he could write it down, he didn't have to remember it. Even this genius recognized his own limitations. With so many things going on in your life, you are constantly processing information. No one needs the added pressure of trying to remember places, events, dates, and plans. Give your mind a break and write things down.

A calendar is a useful tool for jogging the memory. The trick is to use it, update it, and glance at it regularly—at least twice a day. Yes, even on weekends. Your calendar should be your master list for scheduling your time and prioritizing your to-do list. If you don't like the idea of a calendar, then write things down in a place you can refer to throughout the day, such as your computer, the refrigerator, on your car's dashboard, or on a list posted on the wall.

Develop a way to store information in your calendar in an easily accessible place. For instance, jot down directions to a client in your calendar on the day of your first visit. If you need a reminder on subsequent visits, refer back to that date. Or write directions down under the client's name in a separate file and take them with you. Sounds simple. Yet, you may have thought it easier to ask for directions at a nearby gas station, call the client's receptionist repeatedly for instructions, or rely on your memory if you've been there before. Believe me, writing things down will seem easier and easier as you move toward keeping a useful calendar.

In general, it is best to make commitments only after you have looked at your calendar. Some people find this difficult. Here are a few practical ways to let someone know you need to check your calendar before making any commitments.

- "Let me get back to you today after I look at my calendar."

- "I can tentatively set it up. Let me make a note to myself, and I'll call you later to change it if my calendar shows a conflict."
- "Let's arrange this when I have my calendar in front of me. It's at home. Can you call me later tonight and I'll let you know?"

Calendars or daily planners serve many purposes. You can even use your calendar as a follow-up mechanism or tickler file. You can glance at the week ahead to see what's going on. It's a good idea to confirm a verbal instruction or telephone conversation with a short written note. Often people forget or overlook verbal communication, but will retain a written message from you.

The calendar or daily planner should be the basis for any to-do list for both your personal and professional lives. There is no need to keep mutually exclusive lists of commitments and activities. For example, Betty, a middle-aged woman with many responsibilities and interests, organizes her household planner into the categories, "To Fix," "To Buy," "To Do," and "To Call." She even writes down birthdays coming up each month to plan for buying gifts and sending cards. She says, "My household calendar is part of the written 'bible' that I carry with me in my purse."

Make it easy to use. If you use email frequently, you can keep your calendar in your laptop. If you are like me and carry your planner with you wherever you go, be sure it fits easily in your purse and that you can store it in the car in a readily accessible spot.

Remember: write it down in your calendar, and check it often. The written word is only useful when you look at it.

Habit-Forming Tip:

Let a detailed calendar or planner be the basis of your to-do list for your personal and professional life. Only make commitments once you have reviewed it.

Why We Have Two
Ears for One Mouth

Listening to someone talk isn't at all like listening to their words played over on a machine. What you hear when you have a face before you is never what you hear when you have a winding tape.

—Oriana Fallaci

You can enrich your life by listening to what someone is really saying, and not what you *think* she is saying. If you don't listen, you may take on unnecessary responsibility or do what you think someone wants, which may be quite different from what she actually expects. By listening, you can determine if someone is looking for sympathy, an opinion, support, action, or simply your company and a little understanding. You may, in fact, not have to do anything. Careful listening saves time.

Listening is such a tough task that God gave you not one, but two ears to rely on—and two eyes. Words alone can't paint the whole picture. What people are not saying or how they say it—tone of voice, body language, and facial expressions—can be equally important as the actual words used.

For example, a new neighbor asked my friend Laura if she could pick up her kids from the gym for a couple of days while she was out of town. Laura agreed reluctantly because her son had told her of the problems the neighbor's son created in school. Her reluctance notwithstanding, the neighbor went on to ask whether my friend could help put together a fund-raising drive for the local clinic. While Laura was hesitating to respond, the neighbor closed the conversation with, "Why don't you come by Tuesday morning for coffee and we'll talk about the details?"

What went wrong here? First of all, the neighbor totally ignored my friend's body language and hesitant speech. Then, my friend's inability to say "no" made her take on too much. She could have said, "Thanks for the invitation. I know you're new here and I'd like to get to know you, but let me get back to you. Tuesday morning isn't good for me." Because Laura didn't clarify her response, her neighbor interpreted her hesitation as a "yes."

One helpful technique is to repeat back what you think the other person said. It's always good to put a request into your own words and let someone else know she is understood. Had Laura done so, she could have sorted out exactly what her neighbor wanted. She could then have agreed to a specific task instead of giving the impression that she was willing to work on an entire fund-raising campaign.

Another technique is to simply stop the ball while it is in motion. It requires an assertive approach, one that is direct and to the point. Laura could have interrupted and said that she was not interested in getting involved in volunteer activities with her already busy schedule, but would be interested in hearing more about the neighbor's work at a later date when they both had time to talk.

No matter how compassionate you are, no matter how much you'd like to help, you must remember you have your own priorities, your own to-do list. When you stop and think, you have an excellent grasp of how much time you can commit to someone else. Perhaps you will have to adjust your priorities to accomplish a task you've forgotten, or to help a friend in need. Give yourself time to think—listen, review your own plans, and then decide if you can accept additional responsibilities.

You need to understand exactly what is required before going forward. By listening effectively, you can determine what is required and how much, if any, of your time is involved. Listen to what's going on and ask yourself or the other person, "Is there anything I can do?" Then, with confidence and sincerity, respond accordingly, saying, "I understand you need that. I can do this, at this time. Will that help?"

Realistically, you never know exactly what you are getting into when you enter uncharted waters. I experienced this when I agreed to be the Brownie co-leader for my daughter's first and second grade troops. First, I had never been a Brownie so I knew little about the organization. Second, both troops needed a co-leader or there wouldn't be a troop. My children wanted to do it so badly that I jumped right in, feet first.

It turned into a schizophrenic experience. One troop was highly organized by the main leader and I just basically had to show up. The other troop had a lot of conflict between the leaders, even though the kids were having a great time. I clearly didn't anticipate the "people problems" in being a Brownie co-leader and expended a lot of psychic energy worrying and having uncomfortable conversations with my counterparts. I'm now in the process of reassessing my time commitment and expectations. I'm settling in and trying to adjust, keeping my focus on the children and leaving the adult dynamics aside.

The lesson learned here is that no matter how you understand and listen to the needs of others, you still should expect the unexpected and stay flexible in trying to meet your commitments. At stake is not only your time, a precious and limited asset, but your emotional well-being as well.

Habit-Forming Tip:

Listen carefully. Before you respond, understand what the other person expects from you, restate her words, and consider your own priorities before you commit.

In Sight is Top of Mind

One of the oddest things
in life, I think, is the
things one remembers.

—Agatha Christie

Remember the saying "Out of sight, out of mind"? Well, how can you expect to remember something when you can't see it? A calendar makes sense to most of us. To keep you eye on the ball, use a calendar that works for you. Calendars are the most important visual reminder of your responsibilities. Keep it open and visible. Choose one that works for you whether it be electronic or bound, high tech or low tech, hand held or desk top. A calendar is a calendar by any name.

With repetition, Pavlov's dogs learned to salivate at the intermittent ringing of a bell. The same principle can help you keep on top of your schedule. When you look at your to-do list, go back over what you intend to do today, your plans for the week, your responsibilities. Repeat them and visualize their outcome. Let the undone items ring like a bell. Remember that things change—so stay flexible but always on track. If you had to be there Tuesday but your appointment was switched to Wednesday, write it down. Don't expect to remember. If you persist in leaving reminders for yourself in several places, look through them all a few times during the day to be sure you're on top of things. If you need a special place, find a location that you visually frequent often until scanning your calendar becomes second nature.

A busy executive of a large plastics company who was determined to become better organized bought a twelve-month planner and filing system. Then she spent twelve hours getting the organizer organized. The system grew so complex that using it became a burden. Then one day she took her calendar out to make an important phone call. She left the calendar there, open on her desk. She found as she was talking on the phone that she was able to think through the rest of her day because the visual stimulation of the open calendar reminded her of her planned activities. Her planner became her constant companion from that day on, once she made a practice of keeping it in front of her.

The point is to keep your calendar open and visible. Look at it throughout the day. If you are at a desk, keep it open in front of your phone. If you keep you planner online, check it throughout the day as your do your email. At home, keep it where it can be seen often. Keep clocks on the wall and always wear a watch. Seeing time tick away will motivate you to use it to your best advantage.

This tip applies to all aspects of your life, not just the calendar. If you have to go to the dry cleaners, leave the soiled clothes in a visible place so you don't forget to drop them off. The same goes for shoes to be repaired, videos and DVDs to be returned, and film to be developed. If you designate a spot for all the family to leave items and a note describing what needs to be done, you save errand-running time and keep from forgetting to do what needs to be done.

Habit-Forming Tip:

Maintain your planner in an easily visible place. Update it throughout the day. Inform others of any changes.

Clean Up After Yourself— Tie Loose Ends

When you finish with a job, it is wiser to make the break completely. Cut off the old life, clean and sharp. If your mind is tired, this is the only way. If your mind is lively, you will soon find other interests.

—Caroline Le Jeune

A colleague of mine once said, "Thank God for the last minute. Without it, we'd never get anything done." One thing is finishing, the other is finishing right. It's all in the detail.

Isn't it easy to pretend you've finished a task and bask in your glory? Yet, loose ends that are untied are plainly loose. And loose ends are fertile grounds for dissatisfaction. Think of it as *completion avoids complications*. Make sure you don't leave behind unfinished business because cutting corners ensures you'll be spending time later on cleaning up after yourself on the back end.

As I mentioned in Tip 1, perception is reality. Whether a job is complete is often a matter of perception. If what you said you would do is in fact complete, let the other person know you consider the job finished. You need not give someone the option of altering what you've done. Introduce it as the finished product so that no one need get back to you or offer input that takes up more time.

However, if your loose ends are really loose, you just have to tie them. Deal with your trail of unanswered questions openly and directly.

For example, Carole, a sales executive for a large food retailer, always puts her opened mail in her desk drawer. However, she rarely goes in her desk drawer. Often, she's late in paying bills or in getting back to someone because the letters are out of sight. Carole is a good example of someone who should handle paper once. When she opens her letters, it should be at a time when she can act on them and immediately tie up any loose ends.

Loose ends might also be created when you finish a project and then tell the people involved that you'll get back to them on other questions they may have. More likely than not, you'll forget to do this unless you put it on your to-do list. You could also avoid committing to this in the first place. Manage the other person's expectations and constructively say "no."

Always reward yourself for completion and follow through. Don't burden yourself with loose ends. Loose ends only steal your time.

Here are some things to say to handle or avoid loose ends:

• "Well, I've done what you wanted. If

you need me for something else, let's talk about a new schedule."

- "I've enjoyed doing this project. I hope there are opportunities in the future for other ways we can work together."
- "I'd like to do the additional work to answer your new questions, but I'll have to look at my schedule to see how this new project can fit in. Then you can decide if you'd like me to do it or you can do it yourself."
- "The dollhouse looks great, honey. But I can't help you paint it today. How about if I help you start it first thing tomorrow morning?"

For work and professional areas, it's always best to tie loose ends in writing. The written word evokes a sense of finality. For family matters, use a planner or well-placed calendar and pencil in all the projects for the upcoming month. Place it so that all can see and refer to it whenever requests for your time are made. That way, everyone will be able to see all that needs to be done and won't expect the impossible. This is also a good way to mark a definite end to projects and avoid tripping over loose ends. You'll be amazed at the wealth of wonderful activities that comprise your life when you put pen to paper.

Habit-Forming Tip:

Tie up loose ends by telling yourself and those involved that you have completed your end. Anything else needed will have to be handled as a new project, question, or favor. Try to do it in writing to avoid communication mishaps.

Nobody's System Is as Good as Your Own

I think somehow, we learn
who we really are and then
live with that decision.

—Eleanor Roosevelt

How many self-help books have you read?

If you're like me, you are open to lots of new ideas after reading something about how to improve yourself. Yet, those thoughts wane. It was someone else's approach, theory, or method. This self-help book, the one you are reading now, is intended to be customized by you according to your own unique way of living life.

We all incorporate change uniquely. So even these time tips are only as good as you make them. They can only be effective if you make them part of you. They have to fit, feel comfortable, and become second nature. And the only way to make them a part of you is to adapt them to suit your own particular needs, habits, and lifestyle. If it's too hard or too much of a sacrifice, the pain outweighs the gain. It has got to make sense and feel good to work for you.

For example, let's discuss the to-do list. There is no right way to keep one. Here are three different people who handle to-do lists in their own unique way:

- Laura doesn't keep a to-do list at all. She works directly in her planner so she only puts things in her calendar on the day she can get them done.
- Dom keeps two lists: work and play. He looks at each list depending on which part of his life an item falls into.
- Gail keeps a long running to-do list which she updates daily. It's her only source or reminder of what needs to be done.

There are many different ways to save time. Most people find paying bills time-consuming. An entertainment executive told me that she sets aside one night a week for four hours or so, or "until I get it done. Then, I know my weekend will be free of bill-paying responsibilities." A psychologist and mother of five sets aside one evening per month to pay all her bills by post-dating checks. Light a fire. Have a cup of tea. Make the time pleasant.

There are also many approaches to running errands and commuting. Some people find the best way to run errands is to develop resources close to their home or office so they don't have to drive back and forth across town. A colleague of mine sets aside one lunch hour a week to run errands. Some people even schedule commuting time to avoid the worst rush-hour periods so they spend less time in the car. On the other hand, those who spend a lot of time in the car find they can listen to interesting learning tapes, relax to music, and catch up on the news.

Some find it easier and quicker to do things alone. If you are on a mission and have to get a lot of things, let's say, at the grocery store, and then have to go to the post office and dry cleaners, it is faster to do it alone—no kids, no friends along to chat with, just you and your checkbook. Still others use the phone and delivery services whenever possible. Ordering by phone or through the Internet saves drive time and allows you to get more things done in one place and can often be done at any hour. A friend goes grocery shopping at night after the kids are in bed and when the market is empty. I'm not personally crazy about late-night shopping, but if it works for you, do it.

The trick is to do whatever works best for you. Each of us faces a unique set of time constraints and conflicting demands. To fulfill your responsibilities and keep your sanity at the same time, do what works for you. If some time-saving tips feel foreign, adapt them to your own rhythm, lifestyle, or situation. If you're a morning person, do more then. Take bite-size pieces and create mini-deadlines if necessary. Nothing in this book is sacred. Mold it. Squish it. Squeeze it. Make it fit. Make saving time make sense and have some fun while doing it.

Habit-Forming Tip:

Evaluate each time-saving tip to see how it works for you. If you feel pressured or uncomfortable, adjust the approach until it feels good and becomes second nature. The idea is to reduce stress, to stress less.

Do Your Own
Internal Audit

A life spent making mistakes
is not only more honorable,
but more useful than a life
spent doing nothing.

—George Bernard Shaw

In your struggle to keep time bandits at bay, it's important to regularly audit how well you are doing. Sort of like a health checkup. Keep records of your weekly plans for review and follow-up. (Store them in the same place, whether it is a calendar, folder, or box.) Don't spend hours reviewing what you should be doing, just give it fifteen or twenty minutes, once a week. The point here is to trust discipline and not your memory. You've got too much going on, so keep records and give your mind a little break.

Ask yourself these questions as part of your own checkup:

- How effectively am I using my planner?
- Is my planner up-to-date?
- Do I try to do too much in a day?
- Are my expectations realistic about when something can be done?
- Do I reward myself when I complete activities?
- Am I scheduling free time?
- Can I combine a few activities?
- Can I find ways to use the phone or

email instead of spending time running errands?

- Have my priorities changed?
- How can I eliminate some unnecessary activities?
- Do I feel comfortable saying "no"?
- Am I having fun yet?

Once you have honestly looked at how you are spending your time, you begin to subconsciously review your activities and accomplishments in progress to meet your goals. But until time management becomes habit and a way of life, you have to force yourself to do your own internal audit.

Habit-Forming Tip:

Once a week, sit down with your to-do lists and review prior activities to see how you're doing. Be sure to reward yourself for a job well done. Adjust your course as needed. Eliminate. Change. Add. And remember, above all, pace yourself and have some fun.

~ Tip 17 ~

You Deserve a Break

You must learn to be
still in the midst of
activity and to be
vibrantly alive in repose.

—Indira Gandhi

How many things are in perpetual motion? Besides the earth, moon, and stars, few things are in constant motion. Everyone needs to refuel, recharge, and reenergize. You can't race with the clock twenty-four hours a day, seven days a week. To enjoy life and get things done, you must take a break. Make time to relax, refocus, meditate, contemplate, and do nothing. Pick a special time of day—morning, late at night. Even if it's only for a moment, it helps to keep things in perspective. Don't dread downtime, revel in it. Don't embrace chaos, release it.

Here is what some people do when the going gets tough:

"I lay down on the bed for twenty minutes and give the baby a video. It does a lot for me."
—Mother, wife, and business owner,
thirty-four years old

"I make the time for a day when I do nothing. I have the right to recharge my batteries. I read a book and putter."

> —Wife, mother, and stockbroker, forty-six years old

"I do something physical: exercise, play ball, ride my bike. I do whatever it will take me away from what is preoccupying me."

> —Operations consultant, forty-nine years old

"My relaxation is going to the tanning salon and just 'zoning out.' I feel better about myself. I go every Saturday morning at eight o'clock."

> —Administrative assistant, thirty years old

"I pray. I talk to God. I spend some quiet time every morning alone and make my peace with God. It calms me."

> —Wife and mother, thirty-eight years old

One way to take a break from a lengthy task is to do something quick on your to-do list—mail a letter, return a library book, or water some plants. When you leave in the middle of trying to get something done, sometimes it can be a refreshing break to clear your thoughts and take a deep breath. In the end, you can always ask yourself, "What if this doesn't get done? What if it isn't perfect? What will happen if I'm late?" The answers to these questions provide perspective and instill a sense of priority. No matter the length of the break, the objective is to enjoy the process. A little time away can be like a breath of fresh air.

Habit-Forming Tip:

Create mini-breaks in your routine that take your mind off the immediate priority and let yourself recharge your batteries. You may want to do a few low-priority things that are hanging around on your to-do list and that require your attention, but not much of your time.

Resist Temptation

Life is made up of desires
that seem big and vital
one minute, and little
and absurd the next.
I guess we get what's
best for us in the end.

—Alice Caldwell Rice

"If it feels good, do it," is a very short-term approach to life. If all we did was what we want to do, most of us would be piled together on a tropical island basking in the sun.

Well, even tempting things have their downside. On that tropical island, we'd be bored, no doubt, not to mention wrinkled and dried up before our time. In terms of time, the downside of succumbing to temptation is prolonging and complicating what needs to get done. Temptation is a time bandit in disguise. You also must consider the moral consequences and the trouble you get into when you lose your impulse control.

Morals aside, here's an example of a fairly typical list of things you may have to get done on a daily basis, each with a different priority:

A. Prepare tax records
   Meet with tax accountant in two weeks
B. Do bills
   Bills due in five days
C. Write report
   Meeting with customer tomorrow

D. Buy a birthday gift
　　Party tomorrow night
E. Exercise for an hour

Most people wouldn't mind doing D and E. But the priorities show that writing the report is the most important thing that needs to get done. So, the right thing to do is to sit down, stop any interruptions, focus, and write the report. Get it done. Then reward yourself. Go and buy the gift, or combine two tasks and go to the store or do whatever you like. You must resist temptation until the high-priority task is completed.

Another way to look at this is to "do the worst first." That is, do it today. Get it over with. What you don't want to touch should be where you start.

Habit-Forming Tip:

Do the worst first.

⤞ Tip 19 ⤝

Don't Wait

Let me tell thee, time is a very precious gift of God; so precious that He only gives it to us moment by moment. He would not have thee waste it.

—Amelia Barr

Waiting can be a waste of time. How often are you stuck in a doctor's waiting room, waiting to enter a meeting, waiting in a long line or waiting for your child to finish a game before you can leave? The places you wait are endless: the post office, hairdresser, baby-sitter's, grocery store, car repair, ladies' room, bank, gas station, movies, and on and on....

But time spent waiting can also be useful, if you plan ahead. Keep a pen, a phone book, paper, your to-do list or planner, a calculator, and a cell phone on you. Think of all the things you could do while waiting—make calls, balance the checkbook, read a good book, sort your mail, and update your lists. Remember that waiting doesn't have to mean wasting.

If you choose to do nothing while waiting, make "nothing" a time to think, pray, reflect, dream. Alone time can be a replenishing time—increasing your energy in the empty space.

Wasting just one hour a day means that in ten years you will have lost 3,650 hours, or 152 days of your life. Don't let this time bandit get the best of you! Plan ahead, anticipate where waiting may pop up, and use the time wisely.

Habit-Forming Tip:

Anticipate a wait and use the time to your advantage. Have paper, pen, book, blank cards, tape recorder, etc. with you when you think you'll have some time to spare.

~ **Tip 20** ~

Just Do It—
Inspiration
Will Follow

When people say,
"She's got everything,"
I've only one answer: I
haven't had tomorrow.

—Elizabeth Taylor

If there's one thing to remember when this book starts to collect dust on your shelf, it's this: just do it. And do it now, rather than later; today, rather than tomorrow; sooner, rather than later. If a thought enters your mind, act on it. If you're thinking about someone, call him or her. If you remember that you have to do something, do it or add it to your list.

Now, "doing it" doesn't mean jumping in and drowning. You can bite off one small piece at a time. Start nibbling, one small bite at a time. Piece by piece, day by day. Things have a way of taking on a life of their own once they start.

Whenever possible, do it once. That is to say, when you are ready to take action, don't put an item aside or put it on hold. If it has your attention, handle it immediately—once. Then move on. Many business executives handle their paperwork during an afternoon session blocked out specifically for this purpose. Many moms with small children get a lot done during nap time. Many people make decisions on the spot so the only follow-up is confirmation. Put off as little as possible and you'll be amazed at how things seem to simplify. Things can only collect dust if they're hanging around.

In the last analysis, the person with time on her hands has taken the initiative and developed the discipline to make time management matter in her life, striving for breathing space, not busyness. No one can motivate you to better use your time on Earth. It's in your hands. If you want to enjoy life more, you can. If you want to breathe a little easier, you can. If you want to feel harried and rushed, that's possible too.

As the cliché goes, belly up to the bar. Tackle the most important things you have to do (preferably, the ones you most dread doing), limit interruptions, know what results you want to get, and take it one day at a time. Follow up and follow through.

Inspiration will be yours for the asking when you have the time to let it in.

Habit-Forming Tip:

Just do it.

When Someone Else
Can Do It, Delegate It

I think knowing what you cannot do is more important than knowing what you can do. In fact, that's good taste.

—Lucille Ball

It's said that the characteristic that distinguishes a great manager is her ability to delegate effectively. She has developed the habit of intuitively recognizing tasks that truly require her time and those that can be better performed by others. She controls what she has to and lets go of what she can. She places her trust in others and they return it with loyalty and good work.

Delegation involves cooperation and is pure teamwork, with you as the quarterback. You can determine the proper use of your own scarce resources. For example, it's Saturday. You must handle the bills, mow the lawn, and run some errands. You'd also like some time for yourself. Depending on the resources you have available, you might delegate some of the work to your kids. Your son may be able to mow the lawn better than you. Or, if your family left the kitchen dirty, don't clean it yourself. Let the one who left the mess clean it up. Delegating this way will ensure that everything gets done and still leave you some breathing time. And if everything isn't done in the quickest, most perfect way, so be it.

Better to have others learn personal responsibility while you let go of the need to hold on.

A childhood friend of mine who runs a growing business with her husband, and also has two young children, told me how delegating helped her meet the challenges of a particularly demanding week:

I have always helped Jim with office administration and I need a nanny to take over around the house while I'm gone. Four weeks ago, my nanny quit, and we had to dismiss one employee, leaving only one employee in the office for a week. I started getting chest pains. I had no one to help me with the kids. It's hard because I also have twenty-five clients. So I called up four different people to schedule baby-sitting for that week. That took care of the baby-sitting problem for seven days. Then, I was able to have interviews with potential nannies and I picked one. Now I don't have to do my client work in the middle of the night.

To overcome her problems, my friend set priorities and delegated. By focusing on obtaining baby-sitting coverage for a seven-day period, she relieved herself of caring for the children during the day during a hectic week. This enabled her to turn her attention to the other issues: namely, hiring a nanny, working with her clients, and hiring another employee.

Sharon, a twenty-nine-year-old physical therapist, has a husband who travels a lot and always conveniently forgets to mow the lawn. Finally, she asked her neighbor's son to mow the lawn and offered to pay him. Now, the teenager has some pocket money and Sharon doesn't have to do it herself.

Maureen, a forty-six-year-old mother of four, volunteer, and homemaker says, "Delegating is important. By delegating, I am asking others to share their gifts and talents." While the basic tenet of this book is to "just do it," stop and think before you leap. See who wants to help, who has something to share, who can lighten your load.

If there is such a person, delegate. If there isn't, just do it.

Habit-Forming Tip:

Always ask yourself, "What things that have to be done can only be done by me— not best done by me, but must be completed by me alone?" Delegate any activities that will let others shine. You'll be surprised how much you get when you ask for help.

Say Yes to Simplicity

Yes, it is in our idleness,
in our dreams, that
the submerged truth
sometimes comes
to the top.

—From *A Room of One's Own*,
by Virginia Woolf

How many balls are you juggling?

- Work
- Family
- Children
- Husband
- Aging parents
- Friends
- Community commitments
- Church activities
- Volunteering
- Exercise
- Hobbies
- House

How often do you say "I am drained. I can't take this anymore," "I'm running late, can you make it quick?" or "I'm tired but I feel guilty taking a nap or doing something for me"? How often are you breathless, reciting the many things you've got to get done, and exclaiming about the rush you're in?

The things we do to ourselves!

All of your responsibilities, those real and imagined, can push you into overdrive. Not only can you get sick, but you aren't much fun to be around. Those who talk about how busy they are and rush through conversations on the run are essentially saying, "You're not as important as the things I have to do." Those who take the time to look right into your eyes and listen, who let you know they are standing in front of you mind, body, and spirit, make you feel good. You like being around them. Their sense of calm is attractive.

Sometimes, you don't even realize that you are pushing too hard, demanding too much of yourself, until it's too late. You get sick, lose touch with friends, don't have time to help your kids with their homework or read them a bedtime story, and don't have the energy to talk with your spouse about your day. If you are edging toward this predicament, or if you find the time to do everything, but are so stressed and dissatisfied with the process, then it's time to simplify.

The first step to simplifying your life is to recognize the importance of simple pleasures and precious moments. Susan, a vivacious thirty-four-year-old entrepreneur, saw her life racing past her in appointments, meetings, and lists. She took notice the day she missed her daughter's school play. She had marked it on her calendar for the wrong day. When she realized her mistake, she rushed to the school auditorium, arriving at the end, only to find a teary-eyed nine-year-old waiting alone by the door. Since then, she has resigned from two charities and cut back on her exercise classes. She now takes regular walks with her daughter and has established a weekly budget to contribute to each charity. She has made time for herself and her daughter.

What's most precious to you? This is the starting point.

The next step is to consider how to simplify your life. List your activities, responsibilities, and time commitments for an average week. See which ones you can eliminate, which you can share with someone else, and which you can rearrange to a more optimal time. Sharon, an active woman in her twenties, used to stay up past midnight because the house was dusty. Now, she gets her eight hours of sleep and has decided a little dust is OK. It can wait until Wednesday, which she has scheduled as her day to dust.

And you know, it really isn't about dust. It's about all the little things that keep you from yourself—the fears, phobias, compulsions, and impulses not controlled. The one who's too busy to take time to talk is uncomfortable in developing personal relationships—in fact, uncomfortable with herself. She finds it easier to run off and do something than to simply be with someone, have a talk, share experiences. The one whose need to do things perfectly stops her from doing things at all holds unrealistic expectations of perfection that prevent her from feeling good about herself. Simplifying your life starts with getting to the core of what really matters. When you strip your life of all your stuff and the need to get more stuff, you are left with yourself and the ones you love, the ones who make your life worth living.

Then, with the essential activities you've decided on, ask yourself, "Do these things create happiness? Are my family and I better off for having done this activity than not doing it at all? Is there any way I can keep it even simpler, saving time, money, and energy?"

Trying to be Superwoman is an unattainable, self-destructive goal. The few who come close are workaholics constantly battling heavy anxiety, but getting a lot done. You have to ask yourself, "Is it worth it?"

Simplify by doing more with less.

Habit-Forming Tip:

Recognize the importance of simplifying your life by realizing all that's in it that doesn't make sense, doesn't fulfill a purpose, doesn't create happiness and love, and doesn't make you or your family better off in the long run. Then make a list of your responsibilities, activities, and commitments and decide which ones can be eliminated, shared, modified, or reduced. Think about to whom you need to talk to make it happen. Get the help you need to do what's really essential to living the life you love and loving the life you lead.

~ **Tip 23** ~

Seek Support

Those whom we support
hold us up in life.

—Maria Ebner von Eshenbach

How many times do you think "I have no time for myself. I try to keep everyone happy and take care of my responsibilities, yet I am feeling depressed, tired, and even grumpy"? It's OK to feel this way. What's not OK is doing nothing about it.

You may ask, "Where do I start?" Consider any or all of the following ways to gain an understanding of how to balance all that's thrust upon you—and how to make life a little sweeter.

- Go to your neighborhood bookstore or library and seek out books on women's issues, inspirational thoughts, time management, understanding perfectionism, and current psychology dealing with today's lifestyle.
- Talk to a friend or relative who will listen, who has been there before, and who has similar demands and responsibilities.
- Go to your church, temple, or religious and spiritual advisor to seek counsel. Be part of a group or have individual

sessions to seek a greater understanding of your feelings and life choices.

- Spend some quiet time alone and let your spirit wander. In a relaxed state, you will be amazed at how your subconscious mind can be a positive vehicle for change. Listen to your inner voice. Meditate. Contemplate. Pray. Surrender and ask for help.
- Start saying "no." Buy yourself some time to reassess your life by slowing down and breathing slower. Become your own support with this simple step.

You have to start somewhere. An afternoon meditation in her sunny backyard convinced my cousin Marion, an accomplished psychologist with her own clinic, five children, and a loving husband, to change her priorities. During her afternoon alone in the sun, she allowed herself the quiet time to think through why she was feeling depressed. She concluded that she needed to take Saturdays off. Knowing that this could mean a drop in income did not deter her. She needed to spend more time with her children, with herself. Incidentally, she now is a little anxious about Saturdays—she's figuring out what to do with this new free time.

Sometimes solitude is all it takes to discover the answers to our most heartfelt questions. But, in thornier situations, you may not be able to arrive at answers alone. Then it's a good idea to seek support. A friend, a spiritual advisor, a good book, or a therapist may be the help you need to understand your feelings and help you make the necessary changes to live a more satisfying and stress-free life.

Habit-Forming Tip:

Think about what you want to change. If you don't know how to change it, seek support by talking with friends, relatives, and religious advisors. Try spending some quiet time alone. An insightful book may be helpful. As the Bible says, "Seek and ye shall find."

Understand Your Assumptions

We all live with the objective of being happy. Our lives are different and yet the same.

—Anne Frank

Whether you admit it or not, you have assumptions about yourself, others, and human nature. Assumptions are the unwritten rules, expectations, and desires you hold whether you realize it or not. You may believe one or more of the following assumptions:

- "I'm the only one who can do it right."
- "I'm not a good mother if I don't cook every day and keep the house clean."
- "The busier you are, the more important you are."
- "The more you do, the more you're worth."
- "I can do it all: good worker, loving caretaker, loyal friend, community activist, volunteer, good daughter, mother, wife, and sister."

Your expectations may set you up to do too much, be too much, want too much. As part of society, you are molded by the stories you read, the movies you watch, the ads you see. You may think in terms of success and failure, all or nothing. Yet, when you stop to consider what is really important, what really matters, you will find that it has nothing to do with money, position, power, or possessions. There is no correlation between having and happiness. Peace of mind and true prosperity come through the people in your life and the relationships you form.

Rethink the assumptions on which you base your life. How much has to do with what you do and have versus who you are? Reflect on the pace you are setting. Are you breathlessly accomplishing many things while missing precious moments along the way? Are you enjoying your life and spending time with those you love?

Sara, a woman in her forties, began questioning her assumptions about her ability to be a good caretaker. Because her elderly mother needed help caring for herself, Sara cooked for her and cleaned her house once a week. After she decided that she had to reduce the time this care was taking, she hired a cleaning service to go to her mother's house once a month to do the heavy work. Sara has cut in half the time she spends cleaning. She also now cooks meals for the whole week on Sunday and freezes and labels individual portions. Her mother uses the microwave to heat up each meal. Ultimately, Sara found a way to make it work for her and still help out, but not do it all.

The real issue here is evaluating how you determine your feelings of self-worth and self-esteem. You can be all that you are capable of and still keep your sanity by setting some limits and readjusting your assumptions. The essence of this time tip is summed up in the Serenity Prayer:

God, grant me the serenity to accept the things
I cannot change, courage to change the things
I can, and the wisdom to know the difference.

Habit-Forming Tip:

Write down your assumptions on human nature and yourself. What do you expect from people? What makes you tick? What motivates you? What is important to you? How do you derive feelings of self-worth and accomplishment? Then, question each assumption. Is it healthy? Does it come from the bottom of your heart or is it something that you just acquired over time? Is it helping or hurting you as you strive to love the life you lead? The next step is to rewrite your assumptions based on the woman you are today and the life you want to lead. Keep them visible as daily reminders.

Do More Than
One Thing at a Time

You must do the thing you
think you cannot do.

—Eleanor Roosevelt

Computers only know how to multi-process because programmers constructed them to be efficient and effective. No one has to program us, though. It's easy to do more than one thing at a time:

- Watch the news and pay bills
- Talk on the phone and fold laundry
- Cook and clean as you go
- Drive a car and do tummy exercises
- Exercise and read a magazine or book
- Supervise the kids doing their homework and update your calendar or sort mail

Instead of focusing on an activity that doesn't really require your complete physical and mental attention, try doing two things at once. Keep your fingers busy while your mouth and ear are affixed to the telephone. Take your kids to the park and exercise while they play. Do two or three errands on the same route to save drive time. Look for every opportunity to multi-process.

I don't mean you should be compulsive, but you are capable of doing two or even three things at once. When you do, you make more time— time to do with as you may.

Habit-Forming Tip:

Try to combine activities to simultaneously get things done and save precious time.

Make Useful Files

Curious things, habits.
People themselves never
knew they had them.

—Agatha Christie

Do you spend hours trying to find the name of the plumber you used six months ago, the medical receipt for the insurance carrier, or the coupon you got out of last Sunday's paper? If this sounds familiar, then this tip is for you.

Start making files. Yes, I said files. Now, I'm not suggesting that your house should look like an office, but a little time spent in sorting, filing, and storing information is well-invested. It will keep you from endlessly and fruitlessly chasing your tail.

Elizabeth is a good example of a woman who uses files for the most important parts of her life. Elizabeth has two children, a husband who travels quite a bit, and a house to keep up. She has developed a simple filing system that is alphabetically organized so it is easy to understand. Her ten key files are stored in a cabinet in a hallway closet and cover the following: Auto, House Payments and Repairs, Insurance, Birthday Dates/Gifts, Personal, Bank Loans, Credit Card Receipts, Taxes, Home Resources, and Miscellaneous.

As part of her Home Resources file, she files, by type of service, the name, phone number, address, and activity history of the people she uses in such areas as child care, plumbing, electrical work, house alarm service, and gardening. She never has to frantically search for that phone number or for receipts, and can even give out her contacts to friends and family in a time of need. She also looks at her birthday file each month to plan buying gifts and sending cards for the four weeks ahead.

If you can file your papers immediately, that's great. If not, put your receipts and papers in a chosen place (I use a shelf in my closet), let them build for a few weeks, and then file them once a month or so. Don't create extra paperwork, but don't let them collect dust, either. Keeping track of papers will save time in the long run.

If you're high-tech, keep what you need in an electronic file, which is ever so easy to update. Remember that keeping useful files should make life easier, not harder.

Habit-Forming Tip:

List categories for your filing system. (Don't use more than ten or so.) Choose a convenient storage location or use your computer to do it electronically. The most important idea is that the method to store, update, and use information is easy to access and maintain.

Stop "Shouldding"

There is no such thing
as pure pleasure; some
anxiety always goes with it.

—Ovid

"Should" is a word overused by many of us:

- "I should exercise more."
- "I should make more money."
- "I should help my children more with their studies."
- "I should spend more time with my parents."
- "I should make dinner tonight instead of eating out again."

We would all do well to stop with the "should-ding," "couldding," and "wouldding." It eats away at us, filling us with guilt, wasting our energy, and bringing us down. We probably spend more time worrying about what we should do than doing what we want to do.

Remember what's important. If a bed is left unmade or if an errand can be run later on in the week, then stop telling yourself you should do it right now. At the end of the day, no one has looked back on life and said, "What a neat bed I made," "She could fit so many things into a day," or "She led such a busy life."

"Shouldding" takes us out of the present. Life is made of many moments in time. The challenge is grasping them. One "should" you should do is enjoy every precious moment you have. Think of it as micromanaging the moment—making every one count.

Do only what you plan to do, what is a priority, and what it is important. If something doesn't meet these three criteria, ask yourself if you really need to do it. And when you ever start "shoulding" again, make it "I should do this because it is what I planned, it's a priority, and it's important."

Habit-Forming Tip:

Stop worrying about what you "should" be doing by asking yourself: *Did I plan to do it today? Is it a priority? Is it important?* The more the answer is no, the more you let go of the need to hold on to the "shoulddas," "coulddas," and "woulddas."

Work Backwards,
Plan Ahead

Great things are not done by impulse, but by a series of small things brought together.

—Vincent van Gogh

Anticipating what you need to do, what others need to do, and the complexity of an activity is not easy, but common sense tells you what it takes to get something done. Try to consciously train your mind to work backwards so you can visualize the future flow of steps and activities required to complete a project or activity.

Each new day greets you with a long list of places to go and people to meet. Working backwards can be as simple as knowing what you need to do tomorrow morning to leave the house on time and preparing a few things the night before. You'll sleep more soundly knowing that you've given yourself a head start.

Here are a few tips from women whose lives are filled to the brim:

I get everyone ready the night before. My briefcase is arranged, the kids' clothes are laid out, the breakfast table is set. I get dressed while the kids are watching a video, which gives them a few minutes to wake up.

—Mother, wife, social worker, and volunteer, thirty-eight years old

I have a clock in every room to remind myself—and particularly my husband—of the time. If I see a clock, I'm more conscious of time. I even set my clocks ahead ten minutes.
—Secretary, wife, and active church member, twenty-nine years old

I leave fifteen to twenty minutes earlier than I have to so I get places early. I use the "extra" time to review my calendar, take a few notes, or read a short article. That way, I'm not late.
—Writer, thirty-five years old

I use a kitchen timer to make me aware of when I have to start something. I even use the timer on my microwave to set limits for my grandchild. I'll tell him that when the timer goes off, he has to put the toys away and wash his hands for dinner. It really works.
—Artist, mother of two, and grandmother of one, forty-eight years old

I plan meals one week in advance. I buy the food and ingredients beforehand. We usually have a regular set of meals during the week. On weekends, we do different things.

—Mother of six, fifty-nine years old

Every couple of months I look at the birthdays, weddings, and special events coming up and buy gifts in advance. If a store wraps, I pay the extra amount for the time-saving convenience. If I am in a store with a great sale, I buy a few gifts without anyone specific in mind at the time and store them for the future.

—Accountant, mother, wife, and amateur photographer, thirty-two years old

I look a week ahead or more and plan what I need to do to be ready a couple of days in advance. So, for a Thursday event, I may get the things I need on Monday. I also look at times and distance to be sure I can get to the places with time to spare.

—Author and mother of two, thirty-four years old

The best way to learn to plan backwards is to develop a personal time line of the past, present, and future. You have to anticipate your future requirements with your focus on the present. It's a mental juggling exercise of sorts. Remember, smart people plan ahead. And as a wise soul once said, "Time is more valuable than money."

Habit-Forming Tip:

Look out a day, a few weeks, even a month or so in advance. Create a picture of what needs to get done, how it should be done, and what you can do today to avoid any last-minute rush. Make it a habit to repeat this mental exercise regularly. Think of it as a magical crystal ball.

Reward Yourself for a Job Well Done

Though pride is not a virtue, it is the parent of many virtues.

—M.C. Collins

No doubt you do a lot. In fact, you probably do more than you give yourself credit for. Think about all the people you are linked to—at work, in your family, at your children's school, at church or temple, in your community. Whether it's helping a friend out by carpooling for them while they are on vacation or burning the midnight oil to complete a project on time for work or making a meal for someone in need at church, you probably do more than you think. So now is a good time to appreciate yourself—for what you do, not for what you don't do, for who you are, not for who you think you should be. Here are some simple ways to reward yourself:

- Write yourself a thank-you note for all you have done recently for others.
- Make a list of all the things you did that helped others—your children, family, friends, customers, colleagues, strangers—and contemplate how you are better for having touched their lives.
- Take yourself out on a date—go have a wonderful lunch, buy yourself some

fabulous jewelry or clothing, get your hair and nails done, get a massage, don't answer the phone, put aside your list for the day, call some old friends you haven't spoken with in a while, tell those you love that you love them, write a poem, sing a song, or have a candlelight bubble bath at night.

- Start a success diary and keep track of all the new and wonderful things you do, the lives you touch, how others have touched you in the process, how you faced your fears, how you tried something new, how you made the world a better place.

- Don't wait for others to say "thank you" and instead start your own daily affirmations:

    "I did a good job."

    "I'm a good person."

    "I am generous and share my blessings with others."

    "I am thankful for the life and opportunities I have."

External gratification is out of your control. You can't force or cajole others to appreciate you and tell you what you want to hear. Some people don't know how to express appreciation. Maybe they're fearful, threatened, insecure, or simply self-absorbed. Maybe it has nothing to do with you.

While you can't control others, you can take charge of yourself and your reactions. Internal gratification reflects a kind of self-confidence and independence in which you assess your accomplishments in terms of your own particular measure of success. It can be by the imprint you've made on the lives of others, by the fear you personally overcame to complete a challenge before you, the private sacrifice you made to help someone in need. You define the measurement in terms of your own internal criteria of success, as opposed to external measures of power, money, position, and praise.

In the end, the question you must ask is, "Did I do the best I could with what I've got—pure of heart—when no one was looking?" It's easy to be hard on yourself, but far more challenging to reach deep within and appreciate the little things you do when no one is looking. For it is in the giving of your precious time that you imprint on others a part of yourself and, in turn, you forever change the lives of those you touch.

Habit-Forming Tip:

Be kind to yourself and appreciate all the little things you do for others when no one is looking.

Start Your Day Thirty Minutes Earlier

Yesterday is a
canceled check,

Tomorrow is a
promissory note,

Today is cash in hand;
spend it wisely.

—Anonymous

Remember when you were a teenager and could sleep until noon? Now, you're lucky if you get six or seven hours of sleep and luckier if half of them are uninterrupted by middle-of-the-night wake-ups, tossing, and turning. The quantity of sleep is relative. If you experience a deep slumber, calm and uninterrupted, you may wake up fresher than if you had slept for twelve hours. So, it may not be too much to ask that you shave a half hour off your sleep time to reenergize. A calmer, energized you will sleep sounder in the long run.

Try some of these activities in your extra time:

- Write morning pages—Author Julia Cameron, in her bestselling book, *The Artist's Way*, suggests getting up early and extemporaneously writing what's on your mind—whatever it may be. Just let it flow. It's like unclogging your arteries of the thoughts and worries that keep you from your better self, your creativity, and your inspirational thoughts.

- Pray—Set aside some private time every morning or at the end of every evening to talk with God, read the Bible, and pray. Be sure you will be uninterrupted and calm to make it an invigorating, peaceful respite in your daily schedule.

- Exercise—There's nothing like a brisk workout to reinvigorate you. Do something that you feel good about and you will find that you have more energy to start the day and can get more done with the hours you have.

- Read the paper—Do you sometimes feel bad that you don't have the time to do the little things you enjoy, like having a cup of coffee and reading the paper in the morning? Why not treat yourself? You can still do your morning responsibilities afterward, but you have given yourself a personal respite from the world and some quiet time alone.

- Write thank-you notes—Let people know how much their kindness means by expressing your appreciation and gratitude for who they are and by telling them what they mean to you and how they have made your life better. Gratitude comes full circle. Once you put it out there, it finds its way back to you.

- Do uninterrupted errands—Maybe you can do some of the things you normally put off and then feel guilty about because they are left undone when you leave the house in the morning. Maybe do a load of wash, dust, clean, do the bills, go through the mail—whatever you have not had a chance to do because you are a little tired at night. Wake up refreshed and get some of the little things off your list.

- Don't rush—Maybe the half hour only gives you some time not to rush in the morning so you are calmer and nicer to be around. You still make breakfast, get the kids ready for school, feed the dog, shower, and put on makeup, but you do it at a more reasonable pace because you have bought thirty more morning minutes.

If you are not a morning person, try going to bed thirty minutes later. With the extra half hour at night, you can do the things you would do with the extra morning time. Do whatever works for you!

Habit-Forming Tip:

Create more time to do what makes you feel good by getting up thirty minutes earlier in the morning or going to bed thirty minutes later in the evening. Do something you look forward to or finish tasks that cause you stress if left uncompleted.

⇜ Tip 31 ⇝

Expect the
Unexpected

The only sense that is common in the long run is the sense of change—and we all instinctively avoid it.

—Anonymous

Stuff happens. No matter how well you plan, control, prepare, or anticipate, things happen when you least expect them. These normal, everyday phenomena impact your time. Projects are delayed. Deadlines are pushed back. Plans change. So what can you do about it?

The most you can do is to expect the unexpected. Plan for contingencies. Stay flexible. Be open to new ideas. Budget time for things that may come up. Say you are planning to drive to a friend's house for dinner on a Friday night. Why not plan for a traffic jam and leave a half hour earlier or push the dinner back to after rush hour? Why not expect the project review committee to come up with some changes to your plan and budget a significant time for revisions to enable you to still meet your original deadline? Why not plan to cook more food for the party, knowing that people will probably want to bring a friend along?

The idea is to expect that things won't go smoothly as a normal course of business. If you forget this, then you will constantly be swimming upstream and never get to your final destination.

Traffic jams, plane delays, illness, conflicting priorities, emergencies, last minute changes—these things come up. The more flexibly you deal with life's inevitable uncertainties, the better you will feel about getting things done in a reasonable amount of time and enjoying the journey along the way.

Habit-Forming Tip:

Expect the unexpected and build in contingencies and flexibility to your schedule.
The world is not perfect and neither are
our best-laid plans.

Communicate
One-Way

To escape criticism—
do nothing, say nothing,
be nothing.

—Elbert Hubbard

This may sound terrible, but you can save a lot of time if you communicate one-way—if you don't give someone the chance to respond. The best way to do this is to either communicate via email or leave voice mail messages.

Email is a real time-saving tool. You say what you want to say and check the response when you have time. This is particularly useful when relations are strained or you are uncertain about the other person's reactions. The problem is that you have to choose your words carefully because they are in print and because they can be printed out. Don't treat email as you would a face-to-face, for-your-ears-only conversation. We may want to think it's private, but it's not.

Voice mail messages can be used when you know the other party is not home. The drawback is that you have to choose your words wisely as it is recorded for posterity and can be played back anytime. Unlike an informal conversation with a healthy give and take of ideas and sharing of emotions, a voice mail message is fairly sterile and matter-of-fact. You will want to keep it succinct and just get your point across.

Saving time these ways also saves emotional energy. If you are busy, preoccupied, or unwilling to enter into a prolonged conversation, try these techniques. Nothing is a substitute for good, old-fashioned talks over a cup of coffee, but sometimes you've gotta do what you've gotta do in the pursuit of peace of mind. Save time where you can.

Habit-Forming Tip:

Use email and voice mail to save time conversing with someone and yet still get your message across.

Some Stress
is Healthy

Don't agonize, organize.

—Florynce R. Kennedy

Stress can motivate. It can also drive you crazy. The key is in how you view it. All of our lives are filled with pressures, responsibilities, and dead-lines. We all have someone we answer to, depend on, and work with. This interconnected web of relations and responsibilities, by its very nature, creates stress. Much of it is due to trying to con-trol that which you cannot control—other peo-ple. You can't control their reactions to you, their emotions, or their view of the world. You *can* control how you respond to it and how you accept the by-product (stress) as a necessary part of everyday life.

Stress can be helpful. I know that when I have a lot to do, I get more done. If I have a deadline, I tend to work harder to meet it than if I was sim-ply doing something without a time line. The fear of failure associated with doing something new or challenging can be motivating. You are able to rise to the challenge of doing your personal best when the best is expected of you. Here are some daily affirmations to use to underscore the fact that stress can be healthy and motivating:

- "I like to be busy. The busier I am, the more I accomplish."
- "I know that real personal growth happens when I face my fears."
- "I don't strive for perfection at the cost of personal satisfaction and peace of mind."
- "I will agree to do things in a time and manner that make me feel good."
- "Conflict is a normal part of life when there are two or more people in a room. I respect others' opinions and want a healthy exchange of ideas."
- "I know that good communication relieves stress and will strive to keep positive thoughts and good personal relations at the forefront of all I say and do."

Stress can be your friend or foe, your advocate or adversary. How you view its effect on you makes a difference in not only your motivation and performance, but in your personal sense of satisfaction. You may not be able to change the circumstances, but you surely can choose your response to it. Think positive, affirming thoughts and give yourself permission to make stress work for you.

Habit-Forming Tip:

Stress can be motivating when you choose to view it as a propeller—an essential force that allows you to move forward and get things done in ways you otherwise may not have tried.

Constantly Innovate

Do what you can,
with what you have,
where you are.

—Theodore Roosevelt

With each generation comes progress. Speed of information is now measured in nanoseconds. Technological changes happen in the blink of an eye. Models are constantly updated and outdated, retooled and retrofitted. Think of your life and how you spend your time in terms of innovation.

- How long have you kept the same filing system?
- How open are you to new ways of communicating?
- How comfortable are you with technology and using it in your daily life?
- How much do you rely on others instead of doing things yourself?

Your answers open the door to ways to innovate—do things differently—better, faster, more accurately. In the end, you will save time when you find support for the essential and delete the nonessential in your life. Set aside some quiet time to assess the regular activities you do day in and day out. Think in terms of the time it takes to prepare, perform, and clean up. Break the tasks down into activities that may be supported by someone else or performed in a way, perhaps with new technology, that is less time-consuming. You may discover things you are still doing that you may not have to do anymore and eliminate those activities altogether.

Innovation can be healthy when you use it to support your life's goals. When it frees you up to have time to spend with those you love, to laugh, have fun, and breathe a little easier, innovation is essential to maintaining a healthy lifestyle.

Habit-Forming Tip:

Stay open to change.

⤆ **Tip 35** ⤇

Make It Work for You

None of us can help the things life has done to us. They're done before you realize it, and once they're done they make you do other things until at last everything comes between you and what you'd like to be, and you have lost your true self forever.

—Eugene O'Neill

There are countless ways to make time a friend. Use any or all of the approaches, tips, and inspirational ideas contained in this section to keep the time bandits at bay.

Seeing Is Believing—Visualize

Know how it feels to successfully get things done. Walk through the steps you need to take to accomplish a task. Visualize the reactions of others and how you will feel once you've exceeded their expectations and accomplished your goals. Sense the freedom of having extra time because you chose to do what you had to do first.

Creative visualization is a method that allows you to stimulate your imagination to create mental pictures. These mental pictures represent what you want in life. They can use images, or simply capture a feeling or a sense. To derive the most benefit from creative visualization, you need to determine your specific goal, create some form of a mental picture, run the picture through your mind often, and maintain a positive attitude about achieving it.

See it. Make it vivid in color. Make it large in size. Visualize making time management work for you!

You can learn more about using visualization to achieve your goals by reading some of the many books on the subject. It's a good way to start building a support structure for your newly formed time-saving techniques.

The Right to Have Free Time

You have a right to time for yourself. It's the passport to a well-balanced life. Wanting it is half the battle.

Much of what you achieve in life is based on how much you want something, what you are willing to sacrifice to get it, and what you are willing to do to ensure it happens. Think back on how you may have fought for some of the things you have today, and whether they would be yours if your desire had been less intense. Maybe it's the position you hold at work or the role you play with your family as a stay-at-home mom or the educational degree you earned while working full-time. It took time, desire, perseverance, and dedication. The same is true of free time. You must work just as hard to get it. You'll find ways to control the outside influences that steal your time. You'll learn new skills and more effective habits to determine priorities and stay on track. You'll question your current mode of operation and think twice before saying "yes" to any new commitments.

It's up to you to want to enjoy life more. With your free time, you can choose to exercise, travel, think, nap, do nothing, or even work more. You're in control. The choice is yours.

Subconscious Mind Power

Put your mind to work for you. Repeat key phrases, wishes, scenarios, and preferred situational outcomes. Tell yourself that you can be all you want to be, that you can get things done with time to spare, and that you're absolutely determined to have more free time.

Here are some examples of types of affirmations you can repeat to strengthen your commitment to personal time management:

- "I am in control of my life. I spend my hours, days, months, and years as I choose and limit the ability of others to sway me off my course."
- "I deserve 'off duty' time: time for me to rejuvenate, relax, and reflect."
- "I am relaxed in all I do. I am not rushed, late, or frantic. I am able to do all that I feel is important in a reasonable amount of time."
- "I value my time. I choose to use it wisely and don't let others steal it from me."
- "I deserve to leave the office early when I get my work done on time."

Make Commitments to Others

Put pressure on yourself. Let others know they can rely on you, that you'll come through. Tell them specifically what they should expect of you.

By voicing your commitments, you increase the pressure to perform. It becomes a promise that is self-imposed. It is also a way to confirm with other people that you understand what they want. Fearing you will let someone down and avoiding commitments only breed anxiety. Don't set yourself up to fail. Be confident. You'll sail through.

Forgive Yourself: It's a Process

Let yourself make some mistakes. Understand that you will overcommit or run in circles sometimes. This is a process. Give yourself some room to grow.

Being human implies that you are imperfect. You will continue to hit some bumps in the road as you continue to develop personally and explore new spiritual realms. It's OK to hug yourself and say, "You're pretty special. I know you tried and I appreciate it." Then try again, until you get it right. Sure, you'll continue to miss deadlines, do too much, let others steal some of your time, and please others at your own expense. Give yourself a break. You'll get to where you want to go.

One Day at a Time

If things go wrong and your old habits seem to rise again, don't project into the future. Tell yourself today has been rough, but tomorrow will be better.

As in twelve-step recovery programs, the only way to effectively develop new behaviors and reorient your mindset is to do so step by step. Today is the first day of the rest of your life. Take one day at a time. It's scary—all the commitments, deadlines, chores, and responsibilities—but you can do it. Just keep juggling the balls in your hand according to your new desires.

Lighten Up: Make It Fun

Being a better time manager can be fun. Find the joy of change in the process and don't be too hard on yourself.

This shouldn't be a chore. If it is, then rethink your plan and insert some fun things in your to-do list. Smile when you say "no," when you limit interruptions, and when you do first things first.

Enjoy the changes in your life. They should make you feel more relaxed, confident, and at peace.

Others Count on You

Know others depend on you. You are important as a friend, loved one, and business partner. Take your relationships seriously and try not to let them down.

This is not to say you should be a pleaseaholic or family waitress at your own personal expense. Your family and associates count on you to do your best and be there. It's up to you to take care of yourself while meeting their expectations.

Make Time to Do Nothing

Make time to watch fluffy TV shows or read an airy novel or simply do nothing. Put a limit on it, but when you want to vegetate, go ahead. Do absolutely nothing. Consider it a luxury you deserve.

Be the Best You Can Be

You can have more time to enjoy life. You are capable of changing your old habits with the tools found in this book.

We're all rushing to slow down. The fast-paced, get-ahead-at-all-costs lifestyle has given way to a longing to improve the quality of life by having more time to stop and smell the roses and be with the ones we love. We're exhausted from thinking and trying to do it all in a have-it-all society. It's back to basics and finding ways to simplify. You can be the best you can be by channeling both your desire and determination to develop easy-to-use communication tools and behavioral techniques to save time in everyday life. By learning to form healthy habits, you will enrich and empower your life—and have the time to live the life of your dreams.

The gift of time is one you give yourself.

Habit-Forming Tip:

Keep things in perspective: the unimportant vs. the important.

Becoming, Not Just Doing

The present is a gift.

—Anonymous

Be in the moment. Be who you are. Be still. Be true. Be real. Become what you want to be in the life you have. Remember all that you can become by being conscious of the moment and true to yourself. Satisfaction doesn't come from doing more things but from being more, living larger, reaching higher, digging deeper.

Time is priceless but has no price. Time is a level playing field—no strata, financial brackets, economic differences. It is the great equalizer. Use more of it to just be because it is in quiet repose and careful introspection that we discover hidden treasures of hope and dreams. When we fill our time with doing, there is no time for introspection and discovery. Make time to be and watch what you will become!

Make a to-be list alongside your to-do list. Think of all the things you would love to try or take a chance on before it's too late. Maybe it's taking a new class or volunteering at your child's school. Maybe it's getting a makeover or learning a new language or embarking on a new career. Imagine if you only had a few years left…how would you spend your days? How would you want to be remembered? Then become the person you have always dreamed of being. Use your time toward this end—becoming who you want to be.

Habit-Forming Tip:

Make time to listen to your heart and rediscover your dreams. Follow your heart and tenderly treat yourself to alone time, quiet time with no phones, computers, cars, or people. Just be.

Work Smart,
Not Hard

Our life is what our thoughts make it.

—Marcus Aurelius

Imagine how it would sound to say, "I worked so smart today" rather than "I was so busy today." Working smart means understanding your objectives, the required outcome, charting your course, and getting there in the least amount of time and effort while meeting these expectations:

- Understand objective
- Understand outcome
- Chart your course
- Spend least amount of time & energy
- Meet or exceed expectations

Think of it as driving to a desired destination. You can take the scenic route or the most direct route. Either way, you will arrive at your destination. With the scenic route, you have expended more time and energy while being rewarded with scenery, stops, and experiences along the way. The direct route takes you to your destination in the least amount of time with the least effort.

However, in life, we usually do not have one single thing to do. Rather, we are balancing multiple responsibilities and activities. By working smart, not hard, we can balance more responsibilities while still achieving our desired outcome or we can do less and savor each activity more. Working hard is the opposite, it is the quantity of hours expended that is the focus, not the most efficient process to achieve the desired outcome.

The important point here is meeting expectations. Whether it's your spouse, child, boss, or mother, something is expected of you. Once you understand the expectations of others, you can then chart a course to meet or exceed those expectations. Nowhere does it say you have to spend hours, days, or months to do so. It's all in how you chart your course. So chart it wisely.

Habit-Forming Tip:

When embarking on an activity, ask yourself these questions:
- What is the objective?
- What is the expected outcome?
- How can I best chart my course?
- What can I do to expend the least amount of time and energy and still meet or exceed expectations?

Step Back to Step Forward

Lost time is
never found again.

—Thelonious Monk

Sometimes we need to take a step back.

That which seems so important in one moment seems senseless the next. Have you ever noticed that emergencies often fade? With time, we learn that discernment allows us to detach ourselves from the moment and assess situations to really understand the demands placed upon our time.

When we step back and assess the situation, the true requirements, the real deadlines, we discover that we have more time and are given greater flexibility to do what we need to do.

The best way to step back is to leave the situation for a few moments—take a drive, step outside, sleep on it. Distancing ourselves from the demands of the moment allows us time and space to reflect and reassess. Thus, by stepping back, we step forward.

Habit-Forming Tip:

- Take time to save time.
- Sleep on it before making major commitments.

Time To Give— Volunteering

The best way to cheer
yourself up is to try to
cheer somebody else up.

—Mark Twain

Many of us make time to volunteer, whether it is at our children's school, church, temple, or a favorite charity. Giving our time is the greatest gift of all. Finding time to volunteer, if you haven't done so, will bring you great joy and satisfaction. You will find that you are more efficient and get things done smarter, not harder, when you are motivated to make your volunteer commitments. When we give, it is what becomes of us that matters.

Most importantly, remember that volunteering is a privilege and that you must volunteer wisely. Don't overcommit and try to lead several committees or bite off more than you can chew. Don't select a site to volunteer at that is hours away. Rather, pick something closer to home and, more importantly, close to your heart. Be still and you see who needs your time and heart.

Cherish the moments you have to give to others. Know that you are making a difference by making the world a better place for just being you. Doing good will do you well.

Habit-Forming Tip:

Add a to-give list to your to-do list.

Quick Reference
Time Tips

Remember, adjust the tips to your situation and your style! Do what works for you and let the others go.

1. Manage Others' Expectations
- What do I want out of this situation?
- What do the other people involved want or expect?
- How can I meet their expectations?
- What can I realistically promise?

2. A Little Padding Never Hurt Anyone
- Extend time estimates.
- Estimate time requirements for all links in the chain.

3. Learn to Say No to Others and Yes to Yourself
- Pause before you commit.
- Listen to your gut.
- Learn to say "no" constructively.

4. Build Solid Time Blocks—Limit Interruptions
- Look ahead to identify conflicts.
- Work out compromise solutions.
- Promptly contact all parties to avoid surprises.
- Recognize when an interruption occurs.
- Know that interruptions steal your time.

- Firmly, but nicely, end the interruption to stay focused.

5. **The Phone—Your Friend and Foe**
   - Limit incoming call access.
   - Set aside outgoing call time.
   - Effectively use your administrative assistant and answering machine.
   - Develop conversation closers.
   - Multi-process: do more than one thing at a time on the phone.
   - Use fax or email to shorten phone calls.

6. **Be Reachable**
   - Set a pattern for checking in.
   - Return calls the same day.

7. **Help Your Family Help Themselves**
   - Develop ways family members can contribute to cooking, cleaning, grocery shopping, doing laundry, and running errands.
   - Remember, you are helping both your family and yourself—don't feel guilty.

8. **Brushing Your Teeth Isn't Fun, It's Necessary**
   - Make a daily to-do list.
   - Don't write a new list every day.
   - Prioritize, combine, eliminate activities.
   - Continue process to review progress.

9. **First Things First: It's a Matter of Priorities**
   - Am I doing the most important thing first?
   - How urgent is it?
   - How can I get somebody else to do the task for me?

- What's the worst thing that can happen if I don't do this?

10. Schedule Personal Time
- Schedule all of your time.
- Give your own personal enjoyment a high priority.

11. Elephants Remember, People Don't
- Only make commitments once you have reviewed your calendar.
- Use the calendar as the basis of your to-do list.
- Write down all commitments and appointments for both your personal and professional lives.

12. Why We Have Two Ears for One Mouth
- Listen effectively.
- Measure your response accordingly.

13. In Sight Is Top of Mind
- Maintain your calendar in a visible place.
- Update it throughout the day.
- Inform others of changes.

14. Clean Up After Yourself—Tie Loose Ends
- Tell yourself and others that your project is completed.
- Put it in writing.
- Handle ancillary issues as "new" projects.

15. Nobody's System Is as Good as Your Own
- Evaluate each time-saving tip according to your personality and lifestyle.
- Adjust your approach until it becomes a comfortable habit.

16. Do Your Own Internal Audit
- Review your to-do list weekly.
- Recognize progress.
- Adjust your course as needed.

17. You Deserve a Break
- Create mini-breaks in your routine to recharge.
- Consider doing low-priority things that require your attention, but not much time.

18. Resist Temptation
- Do the worst first.

19. Don't Wait
- Anticipate waiting time.
- Use waiting time productively.
- Take materials (e.g., pen, paper, book, etc.) with you.

20. Just Do It–Inspiration Will Follow
- Just do it.

21. When Someone Else Can Do It, Delegate It
- "What things must be completed by me alone?"
- Delegate tasks you don't need to complete.

22. Say Yes to Simplicity
- Recognize its importance.
- List your responsibilities, activities, and commitments.
- Next, list ones to eliminate, share, modify, and reduce.
- Talk to those who can help you make it happen.

23. Seek Support
- Think about things you want to change.

- Talk with friends, relatives, and religious advisors.
- Spend quiet time alone to think.
- Read an insightful book.

24. Understand Your Assumptions
- Write down your assumptions on human nature and yourself.
- Question yourself.
- Reform them.
- Write down new ones.
- Live it.

25. Do More Than One Thing at a Time
- Combine activities to simultaneously get things done and save time.

26. Make Useful Files
- List categories for your filing system.
- Select a file that's comfortable for you.
- Select a storing place and method.

27. Stop "Shouldding"
- Stop worrying about "shouldas."
- Ask, *Did I plan to do it today? Is it a priority? Is it important?*

28. Work Backwards, Plan Ahead
- Look out some time in advance.
- Create a picture of what needs to get done, how it should be done, and what you can do today.

29. Reward Yourself for a Job Well Done
- Write yourself a thank-you note.

- Say positive affirmations every day to remind yourself of how powerful and able you are.
- Take yourself out on a date.
- Assess the benefits of internal gratification instead of depending on others to validate you.

30. Start Your Day Thirty Minutes Earlier
- Assess the amount of sleep you need to get every night. If you can give up a half hour and still get plenty of quality, restful sleep, do so.
- Do something relaxing or productive with this extra time.
- Make time to pray and talk with God.

31. Expect the Unexpected
- Build in contingency plans and know that stuff happens.
- Constantly communicate. No one likes surprises, so when things change, let people know right away.

32. Communicate One-Way
- Use email and voice mail to communicate when you don't have the time or inclination to personally talk with someone.

33. Some Stress Is Healthy
- Reframe how you view stress and see it as a motivating force and a way to encourage you to face your fears.

34. Constantly Innovate
- Stay open to change and new technology to do things faster and better.

- Assess what you are doing to see if it's still a necessary activity.

35. Make It Work for You
- Seeing is believing. Visualize.
- Want to have free time.
- Use your subconscious mind power.
- Make commitments to others.
- Forgive yourself.

36. Becoming, Not Just Doing
- Make time to be alone.
- Be still and listen to your dreams.
- Make a to-be list.

37. Work Smart, Not Hard
When embarking on an activity, ask yourself these questions:
- What is the objective?
- What is the expected outcome?
- How can I best chart my course?
- What can I do to expend the least amount of time and energy and still meet or exceed expectations?

38. Step Back to Step Forward
- Take time to save time.
- Sleep on it before making major commitments.

39. Time To Give—Volunteering
- Add a to-give list to your to-do list

About the Author

Paula Peisner Coxe was born in Los Angeles and educated at the University of California, Los Angeles. She completed a master's degree in business administration at the University of Southern California. She is a management consultant and also is the author of *Finding Peace: Letting Go and Liking It*. Paula lives and writes in southern California with her husband and two daughters.

She would love to hear from you about any time-saving ideas, thoughts on the book, or questions you may have. Please contact her at:

Sourcebooks, Inc.

P.O. Box 4410

Naperville, IL 60567-4410